The Power of Strategic Listening

Laurie Lewis
The University of Texas at San Antonio

ROWMAN & LITTLEFIELD
Lanham • Boulder • New York • London

Executive Editor: Elizabeth Swayze
Editorial Assistant: Dina Guilak
Senior Marketing Manager: Karin Cholak
Interior Designer: Wanda Ditch

Credits and acknowledgments for material borrowed from other sources, and reproduced with permission, appear on the appropriate page within the text.

Published by Rowman & Littlefield
An imprint of The Rowman & Littlefield Publishing Group, Inc.
4501 Forbes Boulevard, Suite 200, Lanham, Maryland 20706
www.rowman.com

6 Tinworth Street, London SE11 5AL, United Kingdom

British Library Cataloguing in Publication Information Available

Library of Congress Cataloging-in-Publication Data

Includes bibliographic references and index.

Library of Congress Control Number: 2019912667
ISBN 978-1-5381-2130-6 (cloth : alk. paper)
ISBN 978-1-5381-2131-3 (pbk. : alk. paper)
ISBN 978-1-5381-2132-0 (Electronic)

∞™ The paper used in this publication meets the minimum requirements of American National Standard for Information Sciences—Permanence of Paper for Printed Library Materials, ANSI/NISO Z39.48-1992.

Contents

Introduction

The Power of Strategic Listening and the Risks of Listening Failure

Organizations that merely treat listening as a soft skill or a public relations tactic cede the most powerful strategic tool at their disposal. Further, organizational listening failures may lead to financial ruin, legal jeopardy, and reputational crises and bring harm to stakeholder relationships and to stakeholders themselves. Following are some recent cautionary tales of poorly executed or absent listening:

- In 2019, a Boeing aircraft, the 737 Max 8, was involved in two major fatal plane crashes five months apart in which over 150 people were killed in each crash. Following the second crash, with reports that a similar navigation issue was the likely cause, the US Federal Aviation Administration came under immense pressure to ground all 737 Max 8 aircraft in the United States. Numerous other governments across the globe grounded the aircraft from their fleets, and some banned them from their airspace. Moreover, reports surfaced that pilots had been complaining for months about a flaw in the functioning of the aircraft's safety mechanism. US flight attendants and ground crews urged their airlines to take the aircraft out of service. A handful of US airlines expressed continued confidence in the safety of the aircraft and refused to lift ticket-change fees for passengers requesting that they not fly on these planes (Josephs, 2019). Days after these events, US President Trump grounded the aircraft in the United States after support for the action built in Congress and the public at large.
- In 2019, Microsoft received a protest letter from employees objecting to contracting with the military. A group of anonymous employees authored an open letter about the Hololens contract with the US Army that states, "We did not sign up to develop weapons, and we demand a say in how our work is used" (Birnbaum, 2019, para. 12). Although the company

representatives stated that they appreciated the feedback from employees and provided means for them to be heard, they are going ahead with the contract. Some employees reported fear of retribution if they identified themselves.

- At Michigan State University, a team doctor was accused and convicted of sexual abuse of Olympic athletes training at the university's facilities. A series of individuals who ignored signs of the ongoing abuse or did little or nothing to bring it to a halt have been disgraced, suspended, fired, and/or sued; as a result of the scandal, the USA Gymnastics filed for bankruptcy (Meilhan & Close, 2018).
- Wells Fargo became embroiled in a massive scandal in which bank employees were encouraged to open credit card accounts for customers without their knowledge, leading to even larger, systemic fraud. The key whistle-blower was fired in 2010. Unable to find a new job and believing she had been blackballed, she filed a lawsuit claiming Wells Fargo had fired her for speaking out against the fraudulent practices she witnessed (CBS News, 2018).
- Victoria's Secret announced it is closing 53 stores in 2019 (following 30 closures in 2018) due in large part to not keeping up with trends in customers' changing sensibilities in the #MeToo era. Critics say that the runway show is outdated, images in stores are inappropriate, and other competing brands are more in line with current trends for more body-positive campaigns and inclusive marketing (Pagano & Hanbury, 2019).

Oftentimes, routines for listening to clients, customers, employees, and other key stakeholders in organizations are underutilized or completely ignored:

- *Stanford Social Innovation Review* conducted a survey of 1,986 nonprofit, foundation, and other charitable-sector leaders. The survey found that 88 percent of the leaders prioritize gathering client feedback. However, the survey showed two-thirds of those whose organizations were not collecting client feedback stated that the greatest barrier to implementing feedback systems was limited staff time and/or resources and 20 percent of respondents said it was "too complicated" or "too costly" (Milway, 2019, para. 2).
- A 2018 research study of more than 1 million anonymized records of internal whistle-blowing reports concluded that whistle-blowers are crucial to keeping firms healthy and that functioning internal hotlines are of paramount importance to business goals, including profitability and limiting the lawsuits companies face and the money firms pay out in settlements. However, whistle-blowing channels are often unavailable or unattended (Stubben & Welch, 2018).

Other recent examples illustrate that some organizations are responsive to stakeholders' requests for listening to demands and suggestions:

- Trader Joe's responded to a petition started by Greenpeace, which garnered more than 100,000 signatures, asking the company to make changes to the store's packaging. Trader Joe's managers indicated in the company news flyer of their intentions to take positive steps to support their customers' requests: "As we fulfill these steps in 2019, on an annual basis, *we are eliminating more than 1 million pounds of plastic from our stores. . . .* And we expect that number to grow as we continue to identify opportunities and take action. Thank you; we're listening" (Hirsh, 2019, para. 7).
- The Academy of Motion Picture Arts and Sciences reversed a decision to eliminate some Oscar awards from the live 2019 telecast based on the feedback of its members. The reversal came on the heels of a growing mutiny. The American Society of Cinematographers (ASC) rebuked the organization in an open letter signed by dozens of industry figures. Also, movie fans blasted the academy on Twitter and stars joined in. A meeting that resulted in the decision to reinstate the awards was described as "very productive and positive" (Rottenberg, 2019, para. 4). The ASC leader wrote in a letter, "We feel that [reversing the decision] would not only be great for the upcoming event but also a major step in the direction of the ASC working closely with the Academy to deal with the larger issues ahead of us" (para. 5).
- The Fund for Shared Insight has created a tool, Listen for Good (L4G), that makes it simple and affordable for nonprofits to listen to end users. About 250 nonprofits are now piloting this simple survey to understand what is working, what isn't, and what could improve in its work to serve people who are at risk of homelessness, who use food banks to make ends meet, people with disabilities, and so on. These pilots are proving the importance of listening in fields where power imbalances between funders and beneficiaries can render silent the end user (Twersky & Reichheld, 2019).

A CASE STUDY IN FAILED LISTENING

Facebook's role in the 2016 US election provides a powerful case study of listening failure with consequential reputational and bottom-line repercussions. During the scrutiny of Facebook's role in the dissemination of "fake news" during the 2016 American presidential election, there was an upsurge in dissent within the organization. *Buzzfeed* reported that an internal group of Facebook employees formed an unofficial taskforce to question the role their company played in circulating fake news on their platform, which is believed to have supported Donald Trump's candidacy. While Zuckerberg was making public comments to the contrary, suggesting it was a "crazy idea," a group of dozens of employees (representing hundreds more) were anonymously sharing insider stories to journalists about the events leading up to the election. There were months of considerable discord among Facebook employees following Zuckerberg's comments. Employees felt their concerns were not being taken seriously enough by senior leaders.

Congressional hearings eventually revealed that Russia-backed content reached as many as 126 million Americans on Facebook in the months leading up to the 2016 election. In addition, thousands of advertisements related to the election from Russia-backed sources were placed on Facebook. In September 2017, Zuckerberg expressed remorse for his earlier statements:

> "After the election, I made a comment that I thought the idea misinformation on Facebook changed the outcome of the election was a crazy idea. Calling that crazy was dismissive and I regret it," the founder wrote. "This is too important an issue to be dismissive." (Levin, 2017, para. 3)

Later, a Facebook whistle-blower revealed in a 2018 interview with PBS's *Frontline* that more than five years earlier he had raised red flags about the potential risks that users' personal data could be inappropriately obtained and misused but said that his warnings were ignored by top-level executives. Further, a 2019 court document said that a Facebook employee had raised issues about the political research firm in September 2015, despite testimony by Facebook leaders that they had not learned about the data disclosures until December 2015 when published reports surfaced (Price, 2019).

In 2019, the social network is negotiating a potential settlement to end a year-old Federal Trade Commission privacy investigation into the ways in which Facebook allowed personal information of up to 87 million users to fall into the hands of the Trump-linked political data firm Cambridge Analytica. That settlement could include fines in the billions of dollars; demands that Facebook limit the way it collects and handles user data; regulatory oversight; or even management changes, up to the level of chairman and CEO Mark Zuckerberg (Scola, 2019).

Facebook was not always resistant to listening to its employees. In an article in *Business Insider* in 2009, a Facebook employee, reflecting on the shift from an open consultative culture to one more top-down and closed, claimed:

> The reason why we were good in the early days was that dissent was allowed and encouraged. That's the reason you go to a startup. That early team was amazing. (Carlson, 2009, para. 6)

Kathy deWitt, Alamy Stock Photo

However, according to the article, the company subsequently became overly focused on public relations and its media and public image. The Facebook example provides a glimpse into the internal warning system of organizations that can, if ignored, be quite costly—in this case, to the employees, platform users, and the United States more generally—and, ultimately, damaging to the company's reputation and bottom line. As employees become discouraged from expression of criticism or doubt, have channels for dissent cut off, or feel dismissed by senior-level decision-makers, their knowledge and insights can be rendered useless to the organization.

LISTENING IS MORE NECESSARY NOW THAN EVER

Organizational listening is perhaps more necessary and complicated in contemporary organizations than at any other point in history. Individuals in organizations as well as organizations themselves have access to numerous feeds of information, competitive intelligence, professional and industry "buzz," consultancy advice, and fast-paced environments demanding continual improvement and change. The demands on organizations to monitor; receive; process; and store input, communication, feedback, and data from multiple sources far surpass those of previous decades. Further, businesses, governments, and civil society organizations increasingly reach beyond local domains or restricted sets of stakeholders. Contemporary organizations are more likely to have local and even global stakeholders who have widely varied experiences, perspectives, needs, and expectations. More and more organizations find that they must interact with and often collaborate across sectors (e.g., corporations lobbying governmental agencies and politicians, nonprofits partnering with businesses for fund-raising and development, and higher education institutions working closely with foundations and governmental oversight agencies). This sort of cross-sector interaction increases channels of information, adds communication load, and further complicates the challenges of interpreting received messages and input.

In addition to complexity in external channels for listening, internal stakeholders increasingly hold expectations for being heard within organizations. It is now normative for organizations to solicit wide input on major initiatives, to routinely conduct employee feedback surveys and exit interviews, to create confidential whistle-blowing channels, and to move toward increasing engagement through high-involvement strategies. Further, new matrix structures of organization and geographically distributed organizations call for increasing collaboration among teams within organizations. Consequently, contemporary organizational structures demand more listening among peers than in traditional hierarchical systems, where conflicts, differences, and variation of interpretations were more often resolved through the chain of command.

CONSEQUENCES OF ORGANIZATIONAL LISTENING FAILURE

As the preceding examples illustrate, the consequences of poor listening in organizations can be significant. Beyond the financial and reputational implications, we can turn to historical cases of organizational catastrophe to further underscore significant consequences of poor listening. Richard A. Clarke and R. P. Eddy's 2017 book, *Warnings: Finding Cassandras to Stop Catastrophes*, examines several highly public cases of organizational failures in listening. Both Clarke and Eddy are deeply experienced in national security and are CEOs and White House National Security Council veterans. They examine several cases where a "Cassandra" provided detailed, repeated, documented, data-driven warnings preceding preventable catastrophic events. Included in Clarke and Eddy's (2017) review are the following three organizational cases.

NASA *Challenger* Disaster
"The launch proceeded on the morning of January 28, 1986, in an ambient temperature of 36 degrees Fahrenheit, 15 degrees colder than on any previous attempt. *Challenger*'s mission ended at 11:39 a.m., seventy-three seconds after

liftoff, when an O-ring seal in the right solid rocket booster failed. The result was complete structural failure. A horrified American public, along with engineers and managers at NASA and Morton-Thiokol, watched as the vehicle was ripped apart in a giant fireball." (p. 13)

Upper Big Branch Mine Disaster

On April 5, 2010, "at 3:02 pm, a powerful explosion tore through the Upper Big Branch (UBB) coal mine, operated by Performance Coal, a subsidiary of Massey Energy Company. The explosion propagated through the nearly two and a half miles of tunnels buried about a thousand feet below the surface of Raleigh County, West Virginia, with a force so strong that rocks, debris, and people near the entrances were ejected from the mine portals. Smoke and dust roared from the openings with a sound, described by witnesses, like a jet engine. Twenty-nine men who were working underground did not survive." (p. 130)

Fukushima Nuclear Disaster

On March 11, 2011, a magnitude 9.0 earthquake shook Japan, triggering a series of tsunami waves racing at 435 miles per hour and "exploded onto Japan's shore with a force not experienced for at least a thousand years" (p. 81). The resulting flooding of the Fukushima Daiichi Power Plant resulted in catastrophic loss of power, explosions, fire, release of radioactivity, and the worst nuclear disaster since the meltdown at Chernobyl in 1986.

In each of these cases, Clarke and Eddy describe the important role of Cassandras (taken from the Greek mythology figure) who had accurately predicted what would happen and provided significant and repeated warnings to decision-makers. The Cassandras were "often ignored, their warnings denigrated, disregarded, or given only inadequate, token responses" (p. 4). Clarke and Eddy explore the specific events leading up to these catastrophic events and the multiple means, methods, and efforts that experts and well-positioned organizational employees took to forestall them from occurring. What is clear from these analyses is that often flawed processes; biases in how evidence, data, and cautionary signals are processed; and the lack of listening are responsible for preventable and sometimes tragic failures in organizations.

WHY DO ORGANIZATIONS FAIL TO LISTEN?

A number of explanations for organizational listening failures have been explored and offered, and I will return to this topic in chapter 2. Clarke and Eddy identify significant and prolific problems in organizational listening in the cases they examined. For example, they describe the *initial occurrence syndrome*, which "tends to prejudice our interpretation and understanding

xii

of the world in favor of information that is most accessible in our memory, things that we have experienced in the recent past" (p. 35). The initial occurrence syndrome is one explanation, they argue, for the poor planning that magnified the catastrophic events of Hurricane Katrina. Experts had warned for years of the likely calamitous outcomes of a major hurricane like Katrina. Because New Orleans had always scraped through big storms before, many leaders and decision-makers as well as ordinary citizens were led to more easily dismiss dire warnings (p. 52). Also, in the case of the UBB mine disaster, "warnings were ignored because the disaster they predicted had never before been seen" (p. 140). Clarke and Eddy argue that, in such cases, organizations will sometimes develop a stance of "institutional refusal." In such cases, where there is such disbelief in the likelihood of a catastrophic event, leaders will simply not accept any evidence, no matter the amount or significance, to prompt a plan or response to a threat. An associated dynamic is in raising the bar for evidence in support of a perceived threat to such a level that only perfect data would warrant action. They refer to this as *scientific reticence*, which they define as "a reluctance to make a judgment in the absence of perfect and complete data" (p. 79).

Group think is a well-documented, flawed process in group decision-making that has long been argued to have played a significant role in the *Challenger* disaster. The Rogers Commission, which investigated the *Challenger* disaster, identified poor communication as a key part of the disastrous decision-making that led to the accident:

> [T]he Rogers Commission interviewed engineers and decision-makers at both NASA and Morton Thiokol, the company that built the solid rocket boosters. What it found was a stunning lack of communication—almost as if officials had been playing a game of broken telephone, with the result that incomplete and misleading information reached NASA's top echelons. And among that ill-translated information were concerns about the O-rings. The issue was completely absent from all the flight-readiness documents.
>
> The Commission ultimately flagged the root cause of the accident as "a serious flaw in the decision-making process leading up to the launch." Seven lives could have been saved if concerns about the O-rings had reached the right people.
>
> It was nearly three years before NASA launched another shuttle mission. In the interim, a handful of changes were recommended—some technical, but most focusing on repairing the damaged communications pathways, management culture and safety organization at NASA. (Teitel, 2018, para. 11, 13, 18)

Clarke and Eddy argue that *erroneous consensus* was responsible for many of the cases they examined. Erroneous consensus involves experts and decision-makers creating strong consensus in predicting that things cannot be as bad as the signals might suggest. Those norms tend to reinforce the usual interpretation of data rather than giving strong consideration to outliers or alternative interpretations. These biases can be ensconced in the chain of command in organizations in ways that militate against examination of non-normal findings or unusual data. For example, Clarke and Eddy found that, in the aftermath of the Fukushima Nuclear Power Plant accident, experts noted that systems and corporate culture that discourage sharing bad news upwardly played a role. Physicist Amory Lovins explained, "rigid bureaucratic structures, reluctance to send bad news upwards, need to save face, weak development of policy alternatives, . . . and TEPCO's very hierarchical management culture" all played a role in the disaster (Clarke & Eddy, 2017, p. 87). In some cases, organizational leaders fail to listen to warnings because of the magnitude of the problem that is being indicated. When feeling overwhelmed by the size and scope and feeling unready to cope, leaders refuse to consider evidence or contemplate something catastrophic.

In organizational contexts, listening is a by-product of organizational culture, management structure, decision-making processes, and design of systems to collect and process input. To improve organizational listening, we need to do more than address the personal practices and orientations of individuals; we need to design better systems and structures in organizations. We need to design organizations to listen.

COMMON APPROACHES TO ORGANIZATIONAL LISTENING

Despite the multitude of input processing demands on organizations, management and leadership advice, consultation, and business communication education tend to focus on speaking, persuading, disseminating, informing, and influencing. Listening is commonly thought of as a courtesy or generous act given to others. Its strategic value is often overlooked, and practical advice to leaders in organizations about how to listen effectively is nearly absent. Although we can certainly view listening as a noble act, we should also consider the ways in which listening is a tool for strategic action within and by contemporary organizations. Listening is something organizations should learn to accomplish in effective, intentional, ongoing, and practical ways. Merely creating channels for publics or employees to have "voice" is inadequate. Voice that is unheard is useless to both the speaker and the audience.

It is not difficult to find books and articles about the benefits of effective workplace listening. For example, some authors tend to highlight the importance of *creating a perception* that one is listening. Benefits are then ascribed to *appearing to listen*. That is, if leaders, managers, supervisors, or coworkers are perceived to be listening, then the people who are speaking are feeling heard, cared for, supported, and as though they are being taken seriously. Such perceptions, if maintained, can then lead to increasing levels of trust, cooperativeness, and openness to resolving conflicts and being persuaded. To manage the appearance of listening, leaders are advised to make eye contact, paraphrase what has been said, express empathy and understanding of what has been said, and ask questions to demonstrate interest and intent to discover deeper meaning. Good listeners are encouraged to avoid talking over, emotional or defensive responses, or appearance of distraction.

Barbour (2016) summarizes the academic literature on organizational listening. He suggests that skillful listening has been related to important organizational outcomes, including perceptions of listener competence, more effective teamwork, and a supportive organizational climate. In contrast, poor listening has been associated with negative organizational outcomes, such as counterproductive conflict and organizational mishaps, including medical errors, misunderstood work orders, feedback confusion, and decreased safety climate. This approach to listening is depicted in the following figure:

Listening → Increase in Trust → Lower Absenteeism → Organization's
　　　　　　　Increase in Commitment　Increase Performance　Long-term Success

STRENGTHENING IDENTIFICATION

This perspective, common in the business and management press, focuses on the indirect benefits of listening in organizations. In terms of internal organizational listening, at least, consultants, managerial advice books, and academic and management journals point to the derived indirect benefits of listening. As individuals feel more listened to, they become more satisfied at work and connected to their organizations. The result of those feelings and identifications are to increase their level of productivity, performance, and presence, which makes long-term contributions to the organization's overall success.

Other approaches to organizational listening are focused on openness to and monitoring of external organizational stakeholders and publics to maintain positive relationships, understand critical audiences and environments, and portray an image of an accessible and attentive organization. Examples of this approach would include efforts at gathering competitive intelligence, performing market analyses, and providing customer and public relations. Organizations will sometimes go to great lengths to create routines for stakeholder engagement, dialogue, and relationship building with key publics. However, Jim Macnamara (2015) concludes from his study of such activity across sectors (corporate, government, and nonprofit) that, on average, around 80 percent of organizational resources devoted to public communication are focused on speaking, distributing the organization's information, and delivering messages. While significant numbers of organizations are creating channels for stakeholders to have voice (e.g., social media), few are creating parallel internal structures or processes to listen to those voices. To the extent that listening is occurring, it tends to have a flavor of listening for narrow bits of information that will trigger scripts of new speaking on the part of the organization (e.g., customer relationship management designed to gain repeat sales or upsell to customers). The point of this type of listening is to better execute original thinking and decisions rather than to seriously call into question those plans. This approach is depicted in the following figure:

Providing → Collecting Opinions, → Creating Impression → Crafting Responses to
Channels   Reactions, Perspectives   of Listening   Collected Input
                                                            for Voice

In this approach to organizational listening, the benefit to the organization for providing channels for input is to determine stakeholders' errors in interpretation and then adjust messaging strategies as a result. A side benefit of this approach is the creation of the impression that the organization is open to stakeholders' feedback.

DEFINING ORGANIZATIONAL LISTENING

Macnamara (2015) states, "Organizational listening is comprised of the culture, policies, structure, processes, resources, skills, technologies and practices applied by an organization to give recognition, acknowledgement, attention, interpretation, understanding, consideration, and response to its stakeholders and publics" (p. 19). This definition highlights validation of those who wish to have voice in organizations (external stakeholders and stakeseekers). Macnamara makes a persuasive argument for attentiveness to publics and the benefits to individuals, civil society, and communities. However, despite its virtues, this definition lacks qualities of assertiveness, strategic focus, and instruction on the benefits of listening derived by the listening organization. It tends to highlight a passive willingness to hear others' assertions for the benefit of stakeholders and stakeseekers. While this approach addresses an ethics of listening and identifies benefits of trust and reputation building for organizations that listen well or appear to listen well, it fails to address the important *functional internal rationales* for better organizational listening design that go to the core of organizational goals and outcomes. That is, what do organizations have to gain through better listening, and what do they have to lose through failing to listen well?

The earlier examples of tragic organizational listening failures were not merely cases of lack of openness to hear concerns and views of experts. Experts were invited to meetings, given forums for presenting data, and enabled to make a case of caution—often repeatedly and in detail. One could argue that these Cassandras were given Macnamara's *recognition, acknowledgment, attention, interpretation, understanding, consideration,* and *response.* However, the listening failures in those cases and many others concern decision-makers' and leaders' lapses in *reaching* for potentially disconfirming and uncomfortable data; lack of rigor in analysis of what was heard; and unwillingness to seriously question leaders' assumptions, plans, and preferred worldviews based on what was heard. Oftentimes, what is lacking in organizations is not a willingness to hear out a stakeholder but rather a lack of good process to interrogate evidence, identify and understand implications, and challenge status quo thinking in light of what is heard.

Further, the act of merely listening in respectful tones (e.g., hearing out the complainer, the doubter, or the minority opinion) can sometimes be used as a rationale for moving forward with the decision in full confidence that venting of minority views has anointed the process as thorough. We sometimes "check the box" of listening and consideration without forcing a rigorous search and analysis of information and perspectives—what a colleague of mine has termed "faux voice" (Sahay, 2017). *Faux voice* involves providing channels for stakeholders to vent or deposit concerns and questions without having the ability to influence the substance of decision-making. By putting on a public show that input was solicited without seriously considering the perspectives that are offered, organizational decision-makers sometimes validate their process without really listening. In light of this focus on active and purpose-driven strategic practice, I offer the following definition:

> *Strategic organizational listening* is constituted in a set of methodologies and structures designed and utilized to ensure that an organization's attention is directed toward vital information and input to enable learning, questioning of key assumptions, interrogating decisions, and ensuring self-critical analysis.

This approach to organizational listening is depicted in the following figure:

Listening → Collecting Input, Suggestions, → Questioning Assumptions, → Learning,
                    Critiques, Perspectives   Challenging Decisions   Course Correction

This approach highlights the *direct benefits* to organizations derived from the information and input that are gathered through listening. Learning, self-critique, and course correction are the direct outcomes that benefit organizations when they listen to diverse stakeholders. This is not to say that the benefits in the earlier two models are not also valid and beneficial—as indirect benefits. Organizations that appear to listen (and especially those that listen authentically) will derive increases in trust building, identification, commitment, and performance. They are also likely to make use of what is learned through listening to better craft messages that will be received as intended. These are useful, well-documented outcomes of quality listening. However, the major direct benefit of organizational listening is found in the content of what is learned. Unfortunately, this benefit is often completely overlooked.

KEY PRINCIPLES OF ORGANIZATIONAL LISTENING

This book is meant to cause leaders and decision-makers in organizations to question the listening habits, practices, infrastructure, and processes within their organizations. The book will lay out an argument for the benefits and challenges of strategic listening and a method for internal analysis of listening capabilities and practices. The book is derived from the following key principles rooted in the definition of strategic organizational listening just offered.

Principle 1: Listening is not a gift to those who are listened to; it is a strategic practice for those who listen.

Listening is being able to be changed by the other person.

—Alan Alda

There is myriad advice about how to "make people feel good" by listening or appearing to listen to them. How to be more persuasive by appearing to listen, how to boost morale by listening to people, and how to be perceived as a leader by listening are typical advisory topics in the management and leadership press. Although some of these suggestions, tips, and programs may be useful for individuals' interpersonal skill building, none of them is about *strategic* listening. *Strategic listening* is the execution of effortful and focused practices that surface unique perspectives; reveal new information; and enable accurate and insightful interpretation of events, activities, behaviors, and trends. Major goals of strategic listening are to surface previous unknowns, question the things taken for granted, and challenge the long-held norms and preferences of powerful leaders and units to ensure quality decisions are made.

Principle 2: Listening effectively, continuously, and strategically is a requirement for organizational survival and the most important ingredient in achieving goal success.

Organizations that approach listening as something done to portray themselves as good citizens, to make a show of engagement of key stakeholders, or as a meaningless routine that rarely alters decision-making are doomed to fail (perhaps in a catastrophic way) sooner or later. Organizational listening, like interpersonal listening, must be an ongoing habit of practice that is nurtured, measured, adapted, and improved for maximum impact on bottom-line outcomes for the organization. Organizations that treat listening as a nice-to-have soft skill or a nicety that merely polishes the public image or internal climate of an organization will cede the most powerful tool at their disposal.

Principle 3: Organizational listening requires attention to systems, processes, and structures that are designed with purpose to gather data, information, and perspectives and to build knowledge.

Improving organizational listening is not something we can accomplish by merely improving the individual listening skills of employees, liaisons, and leaders. Although it is certainly important to align the culture of an organization to a value in listening and to work to enhance communicative competencies, including listening, this alone will not advance an organization's listening capacities. Organizations that are designed in ways that impede critical analysis; discourage questioning of long-standing reasoning; or block engagement with evidence, information, and data, will fail, despite the best efforts of excellent individual listeners. Listeners must be enabled to surface input upward through the organization, share laterally across units, and engage with processes that routinely challenge biases.

Principle 4: Organizational listening is best accomplished through analysis of listening capabilities and areas of inattention; strategically building meaningful listening systems, structures, and processes; and instilling a culture of high-capacity listening among all layers of the organization.

To improve organizational listening, we need willing and able individual listeners who are operating within a listening system reinforced through structures and processes that undergird authentic rigorous strategic listening. The first step to improving organizational listening is for organizational leaders to take stock of their organization's capacity to listen. Once weaknesses of process, routines, and system components are identified, leaders can make adjustments to enhance their strategic listening goals.

STRATEGIC LISTENING PRINCIPLES

Principle 1: Listening is not a gift to those who are listened to; it is a strategic practice for those who listen.

Principle 2: Listening effectively, continuously, and strategically is a requirement for organizational survival and the most important ingredient in achieving goal success.

Principle 3: Strategic organizational listening requires attention to systems, processes, and structures that are designed with purpose to gather data, information and perspectives and to build knowledge.

Principle 4: Strategic organizational listening is best accomplished through analysis of listening capabilities and areas of inattention; strategically building meaningful listening systems, structures, and processes; and instilling a culture of high-capacity listening among all layers of the organization.

WHY I WROTE THIS BOOK

I am an organizational communication researcher, teacher, and consultant and a higher education leader. I have spent many hours in front of audiences of those who run organizations of all kinds—nonprofits, governmental agencies, higher education institutions, corporations, and small businesses. My research concerns how organizations and sets of organizations work most effectively through collaboration, stakeholder engagement, input solicitation, and participative processes. Much of that work has focused on the implementation of planned change in organizations and how communication plays a key role. Throughout my research and consulting career, I have seen numerous examples of organizational failures that are attributable to poor communication. Some of those failures are clearly related to lack of effective messaging on the part of organizational leaders; however, I have come to realize that many of the most significant failures are due to lack of rigorous listening and inadequate systems, processes, and structures that fail to promote and ensure strategic listening. I saw a need for a practice-oriented book on this topic with light scholarly citation that could be readily consumed and applied in organizations.

The book makes the case and outlines the means for organizations to assess and improve their listening. I wrote this book because I want to cause its readers to take a deeply reflective look at their own organizations and measure the degree to which strategic listening is occurring; to appreciate the potential dire consequences of failures to listen; and to be motivated to examine practices, processes, policies, and structures in their own organizations that can be improved. My hope is to provoke reflection and a queasy feeling of unease about current listening as well as to highlight complexities of various contexts and dynamics of listening. I hope that readers are inspired to take action to design organizations to listen better.

WHO SHOULD READ THIS BOOK

There are a variety of audiences who can benefit from this book and the insights and lessons contained in it. Primarily, the book is intended for leaders in a variety of organizations, including corporations, nonprofits and nongovernmental organizations, private businesses, municipalities, higher education institutions, agencies, and cooperatives. Directors, administrators, and C-suite leaders should read this book and consider the degree to which their own organizations are designed to listen strategically. Leaders who find the arguments in this book persuasive should task people in their organization to undertake a listening audit (chapter 6) and identify the practices, routines, processes, and systems for listening that are lacking. The results of the audit can help organizational decision-makers to determine weaknesses in their listening infrastructure and begin to create plans for improvement (focus of chapter 7).

Internal and external communication professionals within organizations as well as communication consultants are a second and important audience for this book. Not every organization will wish to prioritize a major overhaul of listening infrastructure, but those charged with monitoring and tending to the communication strategies within organizations may take lessons from this book to work on targeted strategies and tactics to improve listening.

Third, undergraduate and graduate students who will be future leaders and communication and organizational scholars will find this book helpful as they develop richer understandings of how organizational infrastructure influences listening. Students taking coursework in management, leadership, corporate, and strategic communication and nonprofit and public sector organizing will find this book useful as they explore communication within organizational and management contexts.

REFERENCES

Barbour, J. B. (2016). Listening and organizing. In C. R. Scott & L. Lewis (Eds.), *The international encyclopedia of organizational communication.* Chichester, UK: Wiley Blackwell.

Birnbaum, E. (2019, February 25). Microsoft CEO defends $479 million contract with Pentagon after employee protest. *The Hill.* Retrieved from https://thehill.com/policy/431501-microsoft-ceo-defends-479-contract-with-pentagon-after-employee-protest

Carlson, N. (2009, April 2). Dissent is dead at Facebook, employees complain. *Business Insider.* Retrieved from https://www.businessinsider.com/dissent-is-dead-at-faceboook-employees-complain-2009-4

CBS News. (2018, August 3). Whistleblower: Wells Fargo fraud "could have been stopped." Retrieved from https://www.cbsnews.com/news/whistleblower-wells-fargo-fraud-could-have-been-stopped/

Clarke, R. A., & Eddy, R. P. (2017). *Warnings: Finding Cassandras to stop catastrophes.* New York: HarperCollins.

Hirsh, S. (2019, March). Green Matters. Trader Joe's is listening to customers and reducing plastic in its stores. Retrieved from https://www.greenmatters.com/p/trader-joes-reducing-plastic-use

Josephs, L. (2019, March 12). Flight attendants urge carriers to ground Boeing 737 Max planes after crash. *CNBC.* Retrieved from https://www.cnbc.com/2019/03/12/american-airlines-flight-attendants-seek-to-ground-boeing-737-max-planes-after-ethiopian-airlines-crash.html

Levin, S. (2017, September 28). Mark Zuckerberg: I regret ridiculing fears over Facebook's effect on election. Retrieved from https://www.theguardian.com/technology/2017/sep/27/mark-zuckerberg-facebook-2016-election-fake-news

Macnamara, J. (2015, June). *Creating an "architecture of listening" in organizations: The basis of engagement, trust, healthy democracy, social equity, and business sustainability.* Sydney, NSW: University of Technology Sydney. Retrieved from https://www.uts.edu.au/sites/default/files/fass-organizational-listening-report.pdf?no-cache

Meilhan, P., & Close, D. (2018, December 10). USOC, USA Gymnastics officials enabled Nassar's abuse of athletes, investigation reveals. *CNN.* Retrieved from https://www.cnn.com/2018/12/10/us/us-olympic-committee-report-findings-firing/index.html

Milway, K. S. (2019, January 10). What social sector leaders think about feedback. *Stanford Social Innovation Review.* Retrieved from https://ssir.org/articles/entry/what_social_sector_leaders_think_about_feedback

Pagano, A., & Hanbury, M. (2019, March 1). Victoria's Secret is closing dozens of stores this year—here is why the brand has failed to keep up. *Business Insider.* Retrieved from https://www.businessinsider.com/victorias-secret-closing-dozens-stores-2019-3

Price, R. (2019, March 22). Facebook warned about Cambridge Analytica issues months earlier than previously disclosed. *Business Insider.* Retrieved from https://www.businessinsider.com/facebook-warned-cambridge-analytica-months-earlier-2015-2019-3

Rottenberg, J. (2019, February 15). Academy may reverse controversial Oscars change after meeting with top cinematographers. *Los Angeles Times.* Retrieved from https://www.latimes.com/entertainment/movies/la-et-mn-oscar-snubs-controversy-meeting-20190215-story.html

Sahay, S. (2017). Communicative designs for input solicitation during organizational change: Implications for providers' communicative perceptions and decisions. (Unpublished doctoral dissertation). Rutgers, New Brunswick, New Jersey.

Scola, N. (2019, April 2). Facebook's FTC worries go beyond a massive fine. *Politico.* Retrieved from https://www.politico.com/story/2019/04/02/facebook-ftc-fine-1271618

Stubben, S., & Welch, K. (2018, November 14). Research: Whistleblowers are a sign of healthy companies. *Harvard Business Review.* Retrieved from https://hbr.org/2018/11/research-whistleblowers-are-a-sign-of-healthy-companies

Teitel, A. S. (2018, January 25). How groupthink led to 7 lives lost in the Challenger explosion. *History.* Retrieved from https://www.history.com/news/how-the-challenger-disaster-changed-nasa

Twersky, F., & Reichheld, F. (2019, February 4). Why customer feedback tools are vital for nonprofits. *Harvard Business Review.* Retrieved from https://hbr.org/2019/02/why-customer-feedback-tools-are-vital-for-nonprofits

RESOURCE

Fund for Shared Insight: https://www.fundforsharedinsight.org

Chapter One

Strategic Listening in Organizations

Can listening be a strategy? Can we be *strategic* in our listening habits and practices? In this chapter, I argue that the answer to both of these questions is an unequivocal yes! Not only is it possible to be strategic in our listening; it is necessary for long-term survival of organizations and for goal achievement. Listening strategy, like other strategies in our organizations, serves some purpose, is part of some plan, and is designed to lead us in a direction. In this chapter, I will explore less strategic ways in which listening is treated in organizations and then detail a perspective of strategic listening and its benefits and costs.

UNDERSTANDING LISTENING

In the introduction to this book, I discussed definitions of organizational listening. Here, I'd like to back up a step to discuss listening in general. The International Listening Association defines listening as "the attending, receiving, interpreting, and responding to messages presented aurally" (Bodie, Janusik, & Välikoski, 2008, p. 7). Communication scholars have long explored the role that listening plays in how people make meaning. We sometimes think of communication as merely the exchange of messages—like sending mail back and forth. However, this shorthand way of understanding communication leads us to oversimplify the process as well as misunderstand the role of listening. Communication scholars have long understood that meaning is not *in* messages. Meaning is also not *in* us. Meaning is created through a complex dance of context, history, exchange of messages, language, reading reactions, and the characteristics of individuals who are communicating. As individuals interact, they make meaning together through the attention given to each other's words, gestures, symbols, and actions, which are then interpreted and married together within a given situation. Individuals negotiate what they mean through the back-and-forth of listening, speaking, observing, and thinking, sometimes not even fully understanding what they intend until they see what they've said. Listening then is not a passive receiving of meaning from another. Listening is part of an active social process of knitting together meaning with others.

During any communication interaction, the parties may assess the intentions and involvement of each other. We are often interested in the investments and attitudes of those with whom we are communicating. At times, in a conversation, discussion, conflict, or dialogue, individuals may feel as though they are not being listened to and, thus, perhaps that the meaning that is being made is not what they desire (e.g., that they have no voice). Think of a time when you felt that someone was not listening. You may have thought (or declared) any of the following in that situation:

- You are not being quiet while I talk.
- You are not being attentive when I talk.
- You don't get me.
- You don't care what I'm saying.
- You are not being supportive.
- You are not agreeing with me.
- You are not obeying me or complying with my requests.

On the other hand, the person with whom you were talking may have thought either she was listening or you were not worth listening to and may have responded in one of the following ways:

- You are talking too much.
- You are asking too much of me.
- You aren't making any sense, you aren't convincing, or you aren't accurate.
- You may be right, but there are reasons that I need to move on anyway.
- You aren't making it clear how this relates to me.
- I've heard you out; now go away.

These examples suggest that, oftentimes, in real life we expect good listeners to be still while we have our say and to pay attention, understand what is said, validate what is said, and even confirm and comply with what is said. In other cases, though, we may have lower expectations. When we say "Could you at least listen to me?" we may only need to be heard out and given consideration.

Typical complaints of listeners concern giving energy, time, and consideration to speakers who may not be telling them something they think they need or want to hear or that they agree with. When we grant listening to a speaker, we often prefer that he or she be efficient, interesting, and relevant and then stop talking. We often expect that, once we have listened, there has been a fair hearing and we are not further obligated to engage. Listening takes energy, uses resources, and oftentimes feels like a costly activity.

Clearly, listening is fundamental to forming mutual understanding, negotiating agreements, empathizing with others' feelings and experiences, and developing communicative relationships. As we engage in listening, we seek to satisfy multiple simultaneous intentions. We have instrumental goals (i.e., what we want to learn), relational goals (i.e., what we want to maintain, build, or let go of in terms of the relationship with the other person), and cultural or normative goals (i.e., how we want others to judge us as polite, professional, normal, and competent). Frequently, the latter two general goals may supersede the first. That is, when engaging in listening, we often consider it to be a generous gift performed for others or merely an exercise in managing an impression that we are a good listener. Let's examine each of these scenarios in the context of organizational listening.

LISTENING AS A GENEROUS
ACT DONE FOR THE BENEFIT OF OTHERS

We often read in books and articles about leadership, management, and public relations that it is good to listen to stakeholders. This is presented in the context of relationship or trust building or, at times, in the context of communication ethics. Stakeholders are those who have a stake in the processes and outcomes of an organization's operation. Employees, customers/clients, communities, competitors, regulators, partners, professional associations, lobbyists and activists, media, and government agencies are examples of stakeholders. Permitting stakeholders to have a voice, or enter into dialogue with an organization, is considered an ethical responsibility for contemporary organizations. It is also often couched as a courtesy or a trust-building activity. Increasing opportunities for individuals, including employees, to voice concerns, ideas, input, opinions, feedback, reactions, and the like is considered by many organizational leaders and management experts to be morale boosting and likely to give rise to increased cooperativeness and better relationships with external stakeholders, whose resources or patronage are necessary to the organization's success.

In cases where feedback from stakeholders is expected to be negative, managers frequently use these opportunities to vent reactions and possibly correct misunderstandings or mischaracterizations. In my own research on organizational change, I have found this to be a very typical strategy for soliciting input. Venting sessions and other more systematic attempts to access feedback and monitor reactions of lower-level employees and other stakeholders are not often well designed to make use of the information and input that is gathered. In many cases, routine venting of negative input is used as a parallel process to the key decision-making in an organization. That is, the two are disconnected activities that may occur around the same time. In that situation, soliciting input from stakeholders is a mere symbolic activity that is meant to reassure, or "check the box," that listening has occurred. Individuals have been given a chance to get off their chest what is bothering them and to share their views and opinions. This is often presented as an opportunity—as a gift. If leaders and decision-makers are present to listen, the gift is portrayed as even better. Leaders may be celebrated for scheduling listening sessions with employees, constituents, customers/clients, or others who might not normally have a place at the decision-making table.

A problem with this approach to organizational listening is that the focus is on the benefits (weak as they may be) to those who speak. Merely being granted an audience by a powerful decision-maker or some representative of the organization *is* the totality of the gift. Although these sessions may be presented as opportunities to influence key decisions, often they are merely symbolic exercises intended to make stakeholders feel better about having given voice to their own perspectives, objections, and concerns. When this is the focus of the listening activity, there is rarely internalization of learning, processing of new perspectives, or challenging of assumptions by the listeners.

LISTENING AS IMPRESSION MANAGEMENT

A second common approach to listening involves making a major show of activities to project an image of organizations or their representatives as good listeners. Some advice books suggest that organizations and leaders should develop obvious, public, and routine methods of collecting feedback from stakeholders to demonstrate listening. These methods can be as basic as feedback surveys distributed to clients/customers at points of contact or more elaborate town hall–style events where there is an open forum for stakeholders to speak their minds to representatives of an organization. Certainly, some of this kind of activity in organizations does indeed collect useful input that is funneled back into product development, marketing, customer service, human resources, or other relevant units in the organization.

"Before you continue your emotional tirade, let me know if you're picking up on my nonevaluative and empathetic listening."

Aaron Bacall, www.cartoonstock.com

An obvious problem with an impression management focus for organizational listening is that very little or no real information, data, opinions, ideas, concerns, or recommendations are being processed by the organization. If listening activities are merely for show, what is gathered is not used within the organization. Suggestion cards are not taken into consideration, complaints are not referred for problem solving, ideas are not mined for potential, and new information goes without evaluation. These sorts of activities may successfully manage impressions that the organization cares or that there is an outreach for views of stakeholders, but lack of real responsiveness and processing of what is gathered will, sooner or later, erode those positive initial impressions.

STRATEGIC ORGANIZATIONAL LISTENING

Organizational scholars have viewed listening as an important workplace skill for a long time. The classic *Harvard Business Review* article by Rogers and Roethlisberger (1952/1991), "Barriers and Gateways to Communication," is often cited as a starting point for this perspective in the management literature. However, subsequent focus on listening has been to emphasize its role as an individual skill, a means to career advancement, and a characteristic of organizations (Flynn, Valikoski, & Grau, 2008). In the latter category, researchers have long identified listening as a key component of organizational culture and climate. Benefits of open and attentive communication climate are often associated with employees' identification and commitment to their workplace as well as increased employee productivity (Flynn et al., 2008). The direct benefits of organizational listening accrued by the organization have been largely left unstated and unspecified.

I argued in the introductory chapter that strategic organizational listening is the execution of effortful and focused practices that surface unique perspectives; reveal new information; and enable accurate and insightful interpretation of events, activities, behaviors, and trends. Major goals of strategic listening are to surface previous unknowns, question the taken-for-granteds, and challenge the long-held norms and preferences of powerful leaders and units to ensure quality decisions are made. Given this argument, activity that is merely intended to mollify, quiet, dismiss, or passively check the box in inauthentic listening will not qualify as strategic.

It might be easy to buy the notion that some approaches to listening are more authentic and healthier than others, but it is more difficult to understand how listening can be considered a strategy. Strategy has been defined in several ways, for example, as

- a framework for making decisions,
- a list of basic directional decisions that guide an organization,
- a plan for getting from here to there, and
- a focus on proactive versus reactive.

Thus, we can understand the notion of being strategic as developing decisional frameworks, guides, and plans that help us get from where we are starting to where we would like to finish. Fundamentally, the assumptions built into strategic thinking (and acting) imply that we have known goals and an assessment (at least, initially) of the gap between where we are starting and where we want to end up and there are various means and methods to traverse from here to there that must be considered and evaluated and some subset actively pursued. To take strategic action (as opposed to nonstrategic action), goals, plans, and decisional frameworks need to be connected. Nonstrategic action involves more random selection of organizational (or individual) attention, actions, and decisions.

We should put some caveats around the notion of rationality in our planning and strategic action. People are, in fact, very good at retrospectively asserting their goals (I arrived here, so this must have been where I was aiming for) and rationalizing any action taken and outcome achieved as indeed having been part of a grand scheme (the reason I did that was because I had planned all along to end up in this situation). Whether people actually have some sort of strategic control or focus in their actions, they like to feel as though they do. So we should be careful about making assumptions that acting strategically means that we are purely rational, which is, strictly speaking, impossible. For example, in seeking to achieve a particular outcome, we cannot examine every path from our current situation to that goal, weigh every cost and benefit of every possible pathway, and determine with precision the exact best path. We cannot be perfectly rational. That said, we can make efforts to be rationally strategic. Sometimes, this is referred to as bounded rationality (i.e., imperfect decision-making that resembles pure rationality). Herbert Simon (1991) described this concept in terms of the means that humans solve complexity. Boundedly rational agents are limited in their abilities to solve complex problems in tasks of receiving, storing, retrieving, and transmitting information. Thus, we must satisfice, rather than maximize, the way we think about problems. We will gather enough information, eliminate enough poor choices, and discover a set of reasonable alternatives before taking action. Thus, our plans are not void of rationality but not perfectly rational either.

Thus, we can be boundedly rational and imperfectly strategic in the actions that we take. Organizations can, and often do, consider alternatives, possible pros and cons, and select strategies that they assess are more likely to achieve their goals. My argument in this book is that listening can and should also fall into this category of strategic behavior in organizations. Rather than merely randomly listening as a generally good practice, we should listen with connection to plans, goals, and decisional frameworks. I further argue that the best strategic listening goals for organizations are to ensure that an organization's attention is directed toward vital information and input to enable learning, questioning of key assumptions, interrogating decisions, and ensuring self-critical analysis.

WHAT ARE THE BENEFITS OF STRATEGIC LISTENING?

The benefits of strategic listening fall into one of three major categories: aperture, discernment, and doubt (ADD). We will discuss each of these categories in turn.

Aperture. An aperture is a gap or opening through which something may pass. I take this term as a prime metaphor for the idea that organizations need to open themselves to insight, information, input, and perspectives that bring something new to their decision-making and self-reflection. Wider apertures (openness) are akin to more listening. Organizations need to determine the appropriate strategic aperture to enable them to hear from a variety of useful and diverse sources without overwhelming their processing system. The benefit to a wide aperture is that organizations will have increased access to input, perspective, and data.

An example of how closed apertures can create potential for problems and open apertures can create bottom-line benefit is provided in Dorobantu and Flemming's (2017) *Harvard Business Review* article in which they make the case for why big companies should listen to local communities. Using the case of mining companies and their relationships with indigenous communities, they argue that

> managers who don't understand the concerns of the communities in which they operate will spend more time defending the company against angry stakeholders than building positive relations with members of the community whose support is critical to their success. (para. 7)

They further argue that it is not enough to engage with those who are most supportive of the company's plans. They note that

> refusing to engage with disagreeable protesters or activists rarely works as a strategy for managing social risk. It is almost always better to seek to understand the concerns and objectives of those opposing the investment than to withdraw, disengage, or refuse to comment. Yet many companies assume that if they ignore the opposition, it will eventually go away. Often, however, the opposition gains momentum, the conflict escalates, and managers have little choice but to publicly respond to the emerging crisis. (para. 13)

They cite research that found that one third of organizations' market capitalization is a function of their stakeholder relations.

Discernment. Discernment enables us to perceive, distinguish, or recognize something. As we discussed in the introduction to this book, catastrophic outcomes are sometimes the result of the inability to discern threats. It is a strategic advantage to be able to correctly forecast opportunities and calamities that will dislodge an organization's standing, resources, or critical support. Listening helps us to clearly see what is coming at us. Noticing the changes in trends, nuances in environmental signals, shifts in stakeholder attitudes or needs, or red-flag warnings (even when coming from unusual sources) can provide us the input we need to change course either to avoid disaster or to capitalize on an opportunity. Listening closely to quieter voices, ones that are perhaps routinely unheard by our competitors, can provide us the ability to see clearly what others have yet to discern on the horizon.

We can see an example of listening that provides discernment in the case of the General Mills Foundation. According to Hessekiel's (2018) *Forbes* article about the foundation, executive director Mary Jane Melendez stepped into her new role in 2015, under conditions of reduced funding and staffing cuts, determined that the organization had lost its sense of mission. She embarked on a company-wide listening strategy: "Over six months, the team gathered data from focus groups, digital surveys and one-on-one interviews with employees around the globe, who willingly contributed their perspectives and expressed pleasant surprise at being included in the discussion" (para. 7). Employees set the course for the foundation through their suggestions and ideas. Melendez's team then crafted a new philanthropic framework to lead the foundation forward. Marshaling the collective employee voice, Melendez was able to transform the foundation and make tremendous societal impacts.

Doubt. It may seem odd to think about doubt as a benefit. Doubt is defined as questioning of the truthfulness or factuality of something. When we have doubt, we are uncertain, and we experience that nagging voice that tells us to recheck, reassess, and self-critique. More often than not, seriously flawed group and organizational decisions have come about through an unhealthy drive to defeat doubt and to bolster a group's sense of infallibility and correctness. Checking can sometimes become an exercise in proving over and over the soundness of our own reasoning. However, when we embrace our doubt and set about to counter, question, or challenge our own assumptions, we either validate our original premises and decision-making through a rigorous analysis or discover some flaw in our process or determinations. When we embrace doubt, it can save us from bad decisions. Listening provides us a means to increase our doubt and to start questioning our process and assumptions. If we listen to critical voices, to those who advocate a different path or claim to hold unique information that we have ill considered or ignored, we increase our own doubt. Although this is often an uncomfortable exercise, especially when correcting information comes from an antagonistic source, it has the benefit of forcing us to retrace our thinking, challenge our assumptions, and test the logic of our plans and projections.

An example of the problems created in organizations where doubt is not embraced is presented in Mackey and Toye's (2017) article in *Strategy+Business*. The authors tell the story of a senior business leader of a global financial services firm who was tapped to lead the $100 million transformation of the company. This leader had long been perceived as excessively image conscious, always insisting on receiving good news. He soon created an environment that permitted no dissent and dismissed those who called any of his plans into question.

> As the project deteriorated, the 10-member project team went from warning him about problems to concealing them, because they feared his withering criticism. The frequency of team meetings dwindled, and he began communicating to the team primarily through two of its most pliable members. When major problems emerged in early-stage implementation, business leaders whose P&Ls depended on the success of the project voiced their concerns. They were unable to break through the wall of happy talk around the leader. Eventually, the dominoes began to fall: Employees disengaged, contract disputes with the IT outsourcer erupted, costs ballooned, and customer data was discovered to be unreliable. Ultimately, the company pulled the plug on the project and showed the leader the door. Tens of millions of dollars and more than a year had been wasted. (para. 12)

The authors of this article report on their global research with CEOs about better ways to embrace doubt: "The CEOs we spoke with said that one good way to embrace doubt is to use risk management techniques to increase the odds that what they don't know—or what they refuse to see—won't hurt them" (para 15). They report techniques such as building scenarios, contingency planning, wargaming, and appointing devil's advocates who are charged with surfacing contrary views and fostering a culture of constructive dissent.

WHAT ARE THE COSTS OF STRATEGIC LISTENING?

Strategic listening has costs as well as benefits. Like most things of value, listening strategically in organizations necessitates significant investment. The costs of strategic listening fall into one of five major categories: introspection, noise, vulnerability, expectations, socialization, and training (INVEST).

Introspection. An initial investment in strategic listening involves developing an honest, accurate understanding of current listening habits, practices, structures, and culture. The investment here is not only in the time and energy it takes to assess an organization's listening (a topic taken up in chapter 6) but also the psychological costs to leaders, founders, decision-makers, and owners as they come to own the organization's lapses in listening behavior. An important thread of the argument for strategic listening involves adopting a posture of humility and an openness to self-critique. In fact, to be strategic listeners, organizations must seek to locate their own weaknesses and failures.

As leaders go through a process of self-reflection and lead analysis of an organization's systems and processes for listening, energy and resources will need to be allocated to thoroughly take stock of the organization. Staff time and resources will need to be devoted to gaining stakeholders' perspectives on an organization's listening habits and practices; reviewing infrastructure, policies, and automated methods for collecting input from various audiences, both internal and environmental sources; and examining how the organization listens to itself (intergroup or interunit listening). An example of stock taking that occurs during this introspection is given in Wessel's (2014) *Harvard Business Review* article, "Which Customers to Listen to, When." Wessel makes the argument that

> most businesses spend their time listening to their most demanding customers—not only because those customers tend to be the most profitable, but also because our listening techniques direct us towards the customers who speak the loudest. And we end up ignoring—sometimes not even hearing—other customers who may become equally valuable in the future. (para. 6)

Wessel cites the example of airlines that chase premium customers to the detriment of the rest of the flying public whose needs and interests are likely very different but less likely to be proactively sought.

Noise. Incidental collection of useless, irrelevant, and uninterpretable stimulus is another cost of increasing organizational listening. Noise is the background hum that may appear to be useful or patterned at first glance but, after examination, can be determined to hold nothing useful. As organizations increase efforts to listen more broadly—as they open their aperture—they will inevitably raise the volume of noise. Wide apertures can create fatigue in managing overwhelming amounts of information; confusion when encountering conflicting input; and gridlock when information-gathering units do not have appropriate direction in filtering or limiting what is collected. Investments need to be made in developing fine-tuned processes for identifying information scanning needs in organizations, which will then activate specific strategies for acquiring information. Information that is collected then needs to be sorted, processed, and synthesized so that it is ready for internal analysis and use in decision-making. Part of the costs of increasing listening activity is handling more irrelevant information in an effort to discover the most useful, relevant, and important information.

Organizations with complex environments may need to handle significant increases in noise. A study cited by Zhang, Majid, and Foo (2010) reports that knowledge workers are spending more time collecting information and less time analyzing it. The authors note that inadequate filtering of information can result in information overload, which limits time for analysis, and dumps of information that may provide little useful insight for decision-makers.

Vulnerability. Openness and consideration of alternative voices, input, and perspectives can create a sense of vulnerability for the listener. When inviting others' opinions, perspectives, suggestions, and critiques, organizations must tacitly admit that they may need corrections to or elaboration of their own views and conclusions. As organizations open the aperture, listen to more stakeholders, and actively engage with critics, they can become overwhelmed with second-guessing many of their understandings or decisions. Becoming vulnerable to outsiders is especially challenging. It is very easy to slip into a defensive mode of listening, wherein we question and challenge the critiques that come in. We may feel the need to convince others that we have arrived at well-reasoned decisions and positions whereby our listening sessions can quickly transition into persuasive campaigns or Q&A sessions where we set the record straight. However, when we shift to defense and explanation, we lose the positives of vulnerability and stop listening.

It takes an investment of attention and resources to suspend our own views and, at least temporarily, embrace the perspectives of others. Curiosity must replace defensiveness. Consider listeners who react to speakers in the following ways:

- You haven't said enough.
- I need to hear more details from you.
- I'd like to better understand how you reached your conclusions.
- I'd like to hear more examples of your experiences.
- Elaborate your disagreements with my position or proposal.
- What do you know that I don't know?

These efforts to derive a deeper understanding of a different perspective while withholding defensiveness or critique lead the listener to gather input that can lead to discernment. When we focus on listening to the concerns, unique information, and unusual takes by stakeholders, we may increase our self-doubt. We may come to a tentative conclusion that we may have missed something, we may be wrong, or we may have been incomplete in our analyses. As we discussed earlier, doubt is a benefit of listening. Embracing the doubt created by becoming vulnerable is important. It is also true that the discomfort that it brings is certainly a cost.

Expectations. Embracing a strategic listening design in organizations requires that leaders raise stakeholders' expectations that opinions, input, concerns, suggestions, and perspectives will be sought and the attention to and consideration of that input will be of high quality. Living up to these high expectations is a strategic investment. As organizations create channels, forums, and general access for stakeholders, they will likely make use of them. Once organizations become more available and make leaders more accessible to be influenced, lobbied, and questioned, it is very difficult to retreat to previous lower levels of openness. Thus, this is a decision that needs to be taken with a long view. As organizations adjust their listening activities and outreach, considerations need to be made for how the strategy can be maintained over time and routines for listening will be developed. In other words, strategic listening is not a campaign or an event.

A 2011 study of "pseudo voice" is discussed in an article by De Vries, Jehn, and Terwel (2012) in the *Journal of Business Ethics*. Pseudo voice occurs when a manager encourages employees to share their views about work-related issues without the intention to seriously consider their input. This study found that perceived pseudo voice leads to employees' unwillingness to continue to offer input as well as to increased intragroup conflict. The authors conclude that "in other words, when employees perceive pseudo voice, they stop talking and start fighting" (p. 229). This study considers the practice of appearing to offer genuine listening that later turns out to be false. When employees feel they are betrayed, they tend to withhold further input. We can expect similar outcomes with any stakeholder who is offered a forum for voice to have that opportunity retracted later.

Socialization. A significant cost in embracing a strategic listening approach in organizations is the need to rewire the way we socialize leaders (at all levels). From MBA programs, to leadership seminars, to career mentoring, we tend to reward those who project confidence, operate as risk takers, and express certainty in their own forecasts. Leaders thus may feel reluctant to admit that they alone cannot discern what is coming and tend not to socialize leaders and managers to embrace doubt. Leaders are frequently measured in terms of their level of certainty about anything they advocate. Admitted doubt often makes leaders fear they will be viewed as weak.

As organizations move toward increasing strategic listening, a significant investment needs to be made in the ways in which decision-makers approach certainty and doubt, fact knowing and fact finding, and confidence and vigilance. Leaders throughout the organization must embrace and model excellent authentic listening. Leaders who minimize their own power and status, foster a sense that others can safely convey critique or question decisions, and report and discuss their own errors and the errors of others without lessening trust are more likely to encourage voice and the surfacing of problems, concerns, and challenges that need to be overcome. The investment comes in instilling these behaviors and values in organizations. We will return to the topic of creating a culture of listening in a later chapter. For now, it is important to make clear that this is not always an easy path. Overcoming years of habits and leader socialization regarding listening is not something accomplished overnight. Investments will need to be made in training, leadership retreats, and building new processes and systems that leaders will embrace and support.

Training. Training is an important investment for strategic listening organizations to make across all units and levels. Investing in training to enhance individual listening skills, values, and abilities is certainly worthwhile. However, here, I'll concentrate on training focused at increasing the capacities of organizational units, departments, and important liaison roles.

Widening the organization's aperture will result in an increase in disorganized information, commentary, perspectives, influence attempts, raw data, and other input. Zhang and colleagues (2010) argue that "without proper skills to deal with information . . . people would suffer from various problems . . . such as information overload, inability to locate and extract relevant information and disorganization of information" (p. 720). Being good at taking in information involves much more than being "open" (aperture). According to these authors, there are ten steps required to execute an information task:

1. Recognize the need for information.
2. Recognize the need for accurate and complete information.
3. Formulate questions based on needs.
4. Identify potential sources of information.
5. Develop successful search strategies.
6. Access sources, including computer-based and other technology.
7. Evaluate information.
8. Organize information for practical application.
9. Integrate new information into an existing body of knowledge.
10. Use information in critical thinking and problem solving.

All but the last of these steps precede understanding and using the information in decision-making. Organizations that take strategic listening seriously will need to invest in training in units that are charged with executing these steps. These steps underscore that listening is not merely a passive activity—like a whale scooping up krill in the ocean. Employees tasked with internal or external listening will need to hunt for it, and, as these steps suggest, that will involve knowledge about where to get it, how to develop sources, how to collect it in useful forms, how to package it in ways that are consumable by decision-making individuals or units, and how to assess the relative value and credibility of bits of information.

Listening will often produce highly regularized, predictable input that can be described, summarized, stored, and handled in straightforward ways. Listening will sometimes produce very messy input that will not lend itself to easy summary, assessment, or storage. Take for example stories of those who are served by an organization. Twersky, Buchanan, and Threlfall (2013) write about listening to the beneficiaries of an organization's work. They note a variety of sources of beneficiaries' stories and reports of experiences with organizations. Following are two examples:

> **GlobalGiving's Storytelling Project:** Teams of local scribes in Kenya and Uganda have collected more than 44,000 stories from more than 5,000 community members by asking a simple question: "Tell us about a time when a person or an organization tried to change something in your community." Using a technology called SenseMaker, GlobalGiving turns these stories into data to guide international development efforts.

> **GreatNonprofits:** Often called the "Yelp" of the nonprofit sector, GreatNonprofits features an online database of reviews and stories submitted by clients, donors, volunteers, and others who have experienced nonprofits up close. Since 2007, GreatNonprofits has collected more than 100,000 reviews. ("Promising Beneficiary Feedback Initiatives Across the Globe" box)

Listening to the stories and experiences of the beneficiaries of these organizations constitutes a rich form of information for decision-makers. However, the form of the input is more difficult to understand and interpret because it is largely a set of comments, narratives, and accounts. Organizations will need to train employees to handle nonstandard forms of data and to develop routines for processing unstructured input. Examples of structured and unstructured input are found in both the external and internal environment. Managers will encounter "water-cooler" commentary as well as employee survey results. Sales staff will have access to competitive analyses and customer complaints. Government liaisons will learn about formation of rules and regulations and have impressions of the attitudes of rule makers and political leaders. Training organizational employees to detect, analyze, and summarize all these types of input will necessitate investment.

In addition to information collection, organization, summary, and distribution, organizational units and departments will also need to learn to engage with stakeholders in meaningful ways. In some cases, listening occurs in proactive outreach-seeking input, feedback, and information. In other cases, listening occurs in a context of ongoing events and streams of interaction and even during crises. For organizations to gain the advantages of discernment and doubt through strategic listening, they will need to train employees to be excellent at listening through unexpected situations and difficult circumstances.

A poignant example, recently in the news, is the case of Alyssa Gilderhus, a patient at the world-renowned Mayo Clinic (see Case Box 1.1). Alyssa was brought to the Mayo Clinic for treatment for a life-threatening brain aneurysm. After successful surgeries saved her life, the relationship between Alyssa's family and the care team at Mayo deteriorated. Conflicts over medication; treatment; confidentiality; and the manner that nurses, doctors, and other staff interacted with the family increased over several weeks. The situation worsened to the point that the mother was banned from the hospital, other family members were discouraged from visiting, and the hospital pursued a court-ordered guardian for Alyssa seemingly to retaliate against the mother for her argumentative stance against the doctors. According to a CNN report (Cohen & Bonifield, 2018), a professor at the University of North Carolina School of Law who was interviewed about the case stated, "'It's confusing to me why this went off the rails so horribly'" (para. 16). Further, Art Caplan, head of the Division of Medical Ethics at the New York University School of Medicine, also reviewed the case and remarked, "'This should never have happened,' he said. 'This is a cautionary tale'" (para. 18). In many ways, it is a cautionary tale of poor listening in an organization that failed to detect a pattern of a patient and her family repeatedly feeling unheard and by numerous staff and departments across the hospital. As Alyssa's mother stated in an early Facebook post after things started to go badly, "'We just need someone who will at least listen to us and hear us'" (para. 50).

CASE BOX 1.1: MAYO CLINIC CRISIS

Alyssa's parents say their daughter's breathing tube was the wrong size and they had to pester doctors to get it corrected. They also say the family—not doctors—discovered that she had a bladder infection. They say a social worker discussed private financial information within earshot of visiting friends and relatives. Her parents asked for the social worker and a doctor to be replaced.

Alyssa's parents say that, at their request, they had a meeting with her care team. "'I had two whiteboards filled up with questions left unanswered, tests left undone, and every other question we could think of,' Amber wrote on her Facebook page that day" (Cohen & Bonifield,

2018, para. 52). On the day after that meeting, Amber got into a disagreement with a nursing aide and asked to have her removed from her daughter's care team. She was the fourth staffer the family had asked to be replaced in just three weeks.

After overhearing a conversation with a social worker and a doctor pertaining to her daughter, Alyssa's mom requested to be included in the conversation. A verbally aggressive conversation ensued wherein Alyssa's mom stated that "'I need to talk to you. Do you understand me?' The doctor walked away" (para. 63, 64). Later, a social worker would tell police that "'Amber interrupted a meeting because Amber was upset over the care Alyssa was receiving. Due to that incident, Amber was escorted off of [Mayo] property'" (para. 69). Later, the family asked the doctor whether they could speak to his supervisor, and they were told, "'I run this whole floor,' and [he] turned around and walked out of the room" (para. 91).

Alyssa was increasingly isolated from her parents, friends, and family as the hospital barred the mother from the facility, discouraged or disallowed visitors, kept her under surveillance, and eventually took steps to make Alyssa a ward of the state (in an effort to disempower the parents' voice in her care). The parents asked to speak to a patient advocate and were told "'there is no patient advocate'" (para. 72).

After unanswered complaints and requests by the parents and the eighteen-year-old patient, the family arranged to spirit Alyssa away from the hospital under the pretense of meeting an elderly relative in the parking lot.

Adapted from Cohen, E., & Bonifield, J. (2018, August 13). Escape from the Mayo Clinic: Teen accuses world-famous hospital of "medical kidnapping." CNN Health. Retrieved from https://www.cnn.com/2018/08/13/health/mayo-clinic-escape-1-eprise/index.html.

One could certainly find much to critique in the apparent communication and listening skills among staff who dealt with Alyssa's family. Blame, too, could doubtlessly be shared by some of the family members who might not have approached staff in the best way at all times (although one would assume that a trained medical staff would be accustomed to coping with family members who are under extreme stress and emotional strain). Aside from the individual skill deficits, we can also observe severe inadequacies in the ways this *organization* failed to listen. That is, clearly, over the days and weeks that Alyssa was at the Mayo Clinic, there were numerous opportunities for various departments and units within the hospital to notice that the family was feeling unheard and had concerns and complaints to express—expressions that could have resulted in learning and adaptation by the organization. As you read the detailed story, it becomes clear that there were opportunities for trained staff to have intervened in noticing the slow-rolling situation as it was evolving into a full-blown crisis. The press accounts include acknowledgment of involvement by nursing staff, supervising doctors, social workers, security personnel, and legal counsel in the hospital. Staff listening training in any or all of these areas of specialty could have helped this organization recognize the listening failures, select an appropriate intervention, devise a strategy to improve the execution of listening across the organization's points of contact with the family, and work toward learning what was needed to become known within the hospital about this particular patient's desires and condition. It was later revealed that the hospital did have an ethics committee—set up to handle conflicts, such as the one Alyssa's family was experiencing—that was not activated throughout her time in the hospital. Strong training of various personnel in handling the overall organization's listening response to key stakeholders is a key to avoiding crises such as this.

CONCLUSION

Organizational listening can be done in strategic ways and be a part of an overall strategy to enable organizations and their leaders to learn what they need to know to make better decisions, course-correct their own plans, and enable thoughtful consideration of the perspectives of diverse stakeholders as they move toward goals. There are several important benefits to taking a strategic approach to listening. Organizations benefit from wider apertures that draw in new information, perspectives, viewpoints, and arguments. The learning that can be derived from gathering input from stakeholders enables discernment and doubt to help leaders to have access to forewarning of opportunities and potential catastrophes and to develop a healthy skepticism of their own analyses, assumptions, and decision criteria. The benefits of strategic listening also require investments. Organizations cannot simply decide to "listen more" and expect results. Investments in the ways in which listening occurs and how what is learned is utilized in the organization will require adjustments in thinking, values, skills, and processes in order to make strategic use of what is heard.

REFERENCES

Bodie, G. D., Janusik, L. A., & Välikoski, T.-R. (2008). *Priorities of listening research: Four interrelated initiatives*. [White paper]. International Listening Association. Retrieved from https://www.listen.org/resources/Documents/White_Paper_PrioritiesResearch.pdf

Cohen, E., & Bonifield, J. (2018, August 17). Escape from the Mayo Clinic: Teen accuses world-famous hospital of "medical kidnapping." *CNN Health*. Retrieved from https://www.cnn.com/2018/08/13/health/mayo-clinic-escape-1-eprise/index.html

De Vries, G., Jehn, K. A., & Terwel, B. W. (2012). When employees stop talking and start fighting: The detrimental effects of pseudo voice in organizations. *Journal of Business Ethics*, *105*(2), 221–230.

Dorobantu, S., & Flemming, D. (2017, November 10). It's never been more important for big companies to listen to local communities. *Harvard Business Review*. Retrieved from https://hbr.org/2017/11/its-never-been-more-important-for-big-companies-to-listen-to-local-communities

Flynn, J., Valikoski, T.-R., & Grau, J. (2008). Listening in the business context: Reviewing the state of research. *International Journal of Listening*, *22*(2), 141–151.

Hessekiel, D. (2018, August 1). Leveraging the employee voice to advance corporate purpose: The General Mills story. *Forbes*. Retrieved from https://www.forbes.com/sites/davidhessekiel/2018/08/01/leveraging-the-employee-voice-to-advance-corporate-purpose-the-general-mills-story/#1d7b2ac4715e

Mackey, J., & Toye, S. (2017, November 29). How leaders and their teams can stop executive hubris: Building a culture of critical thinking and humility can spare companies from the ravages of excessive CEO confidence. *Strategy+Business*. Retrieved from https://www.strategy-business.com/article/How-Leaders-and-Their-Teams-Can-Stop-Executive-Hubris?gko=112ac

Rogers, C. R., & Roethlisberger, F. J. (1991, November). Barriers and gateways to communication. *Harvard Business Review*. (Original work published in 1952). Retrieved from https://hbr.org/1991/11/barriers-and-gateways-to-communication

Twersky, F., Buchanan, P., & Threlfall, V. (2013). Listening to those who matter most, the beneficiaries. *Stanford Social Innovation Review*. Retrieved from https://ssir.org/articles/entry/listening_to_those_who_matter_most_the_beneficiaries

Wessel, M. (2014, April 7). Which customers to listen to, when. *Harvard Business Review*. Retrieved from https://hbr.org/2014/04/which-customers-to-listen-to-when

Zhang, X., Majid, S., & Foo, S. (2010). Environmental scanning: An application of information literacy skills at the workplace. *Journal of Information Science*, *36*(6), 719–732.

FURTHER READING

Simon, H. A. (1991). Bounded rationality and organizational learning. *Organization Science*, *2*(1), 125–134.

OTHER RESOURCES

GlobalGiving's Storytelling Project: https://www.globalgiving.org/storytelling/
GreatNonprofits: https://greatnonprofits.org/

Chapter Two

Obstructions to Listening

The beginning point for designing a listening organization is in appreciating the obstructions that prevent strategic listening. Many consultants, scholars, and advice givers from a variety of backgrounds have written about improving individuals' capacities for quality listening. There is an abundance of resources (see Further Reading list at the end of the chapter) for developing individuals' appreciation for the importance of listening, orientation to empathetic listening, skills in retaining what is heard, activities to improve listening in various contexts, and instruments for assessing listening skills and values, among many others. However, the focus of this book is in recognizing the challenges in an *organization's capacity* for listening. Given the focus of this book, I will not review the listening skills literature. In this chapter, I will present an overview of organizational dynamics that tend to interfere with quality and strategic listening. Still, the point needs to be made that no organizational design will remediate the unwillingness and incapacity of individuals to listen well. Further, the reverse is also true. Even if organizations are filled with willing and able listeners, given the obstructions present in them, they may still fail to listen well. In the following sections, I will describe key practices and orientations in organizations that obstruct listening and appear, at times, to be designed to disable listening.

DISCOURAGING, SUBMERGING, AND DISREGARDING VOICE

Organizations sometimes send strong signals that they do not wish to hear what stakeholders have to say, and, in some cases, those charged with listening activity edit, modify, revise, and sanitize what they hear as they pass along reports to higher-level decision-makers. If an organization does not want to listen to stakeholders, it can make it very difficult for voices to be raised or channeled to an empowered decision-maker.

In my own research into how organizations implement change, my co-investigator and I interviewed individuals tasked with soliciting input during a major organizational change (Lewis & Russ, 2012). Our interviewees were from organizations in New York City, which represented a diverse range of industries, including health care, retail, professional services, food and beverage, insurance, legal, manufacturing, and finance. The average size of participants' organizations was 44,000 employees (range was 3,000–118,000 employees). We found that, when leaders sought input about ongoing change initiatives, they often used a "restricted" model, which involved seeking input from a very select group of stakeholders, and did so in ways that confirmed implementers' original decisions. Leaders who adopted this general style influenced those charged with collecting and vetting input. Often, the result was the use of defensive strategies to prevent some types of feedback from reaching decision-makers. Collected input was frequently dismissed when there were no ready solutions to raised problems. Also, unique information that had not been endorsed widely was often discarded:

> "I tried to do a check and make sure this feedback would also be relevant to a greater general population. If it was, I tried to incorporate it. If it was just unique to this group, then I decided to disregard it." As Fiona reported, "I would prob-ably just go with the majority . . . because I feel the feedback is probably more validated." (p. 277)

Highly critical input was often characterized as "lashing out," "venting," or a product of general "unhappiness" of the provider. Some individuals' input was dismissed because people were deemed to be disgruntled in general who were merely lashing out in their feedback about change:

> "I'm going to take what I need and let the rest go." In addition, Beth stated, "I mean some [people just] worry; some people just aren't happy people." (p. 278)

Interviews with implementers revealed that these approaches were due to an adopted style of leadership wherein fidelity to original plans was valued more than any desire to mine the insights of internal and external stakeholders for insight or critique.

Those tasked with gathering input tended to seek out individuals who were deemed "knowledgeable and savvy," "successful," or "high performers" (p. 277) or those who were considered "thought leaders" and "advocates" and who would "help support the change" (p. 279). In general, we found that input was sought from those who were more favorable to change:

> "I would find myself energized and refreshed when I would meet with those people. And then they would be informed about the effort and inclined to support it and so I was actually getting the work done but I was also getting restored personally." (p. 279)

The approaches to seeking input during change initiatives tended to follow a mode of dismissing or disregarding as much inconvenient information and perspectives as possible. In our article, we speculated that this strategy might have been partly due to the role these particular input collectors played in their organizations. We interviewed human resource professionals, who are often charged to collect input about change programs. It may be that those in the middle of organizations, tasked by those at the top to gather input, try very hard not to surface problems that cannot be easily solved:

> [T]hey have been tasked with making a change happen and using their "people skills" to execute the decisions of upper management. Consequently, they may hesitate in running unresolved "people problems" up the chain of command for fear of diminishing their perceived competence, status, and standing in the organization as qualified HR experts. Our interviewees may feel that if they can forestall stakeholders' complaining, dismiss their criticisms, or reorient their negative thinking/feelings, they may be better able to craft a successful image for themselves, strengthen their perceived role within the organization, and validate their status as HR professionals. (Lewis & Russ, 2012, p. 286)

Certainly, communication practices like those described here help explain why some who offer their voices are ultimately ignored. Another example with similar dynamics is provided in a customer service case by Macnamara (2014), who describes an insurance company that had handled a claim in a grudging and unsatisfactory way. Following the resolution of the claim, the company sent an email requesting customer feedback:

> The email listed only one question with a five-point Likert scale offering a choice of "awesome, good, acceptable, bad, very bad" [personal communication April 11, 2015] . . . the online link for "feedback" provided no opportunity to enter comments—only a single choice to click one of the options on the five-point scale. Also, despite having dealt with several staff during the claim process, there was no opportunity to rate anyone other than the initial contact whose name was pre-entered on the feedback form. This is hardly listening to customers. All customer engagement was framed within tightly scripted or rehearsed statements and limited choices. (p. 144)

Macnamara goes on to describe how the attempts to reply with any type of unscripted commentary was prevented by the company. Reply emails sent to the company's email received "bounce back" messages. Attempts to use the online "wall" on the company website under the tab "Feedback," which states "Have Your Say—we're listening," repeatedly produced error messages when comments were submitted. Macnamara concluded, "The company's systems and processes ensured, either intentionally or unintentionally, that it heard what it wanted to hear—and nothing else" (p. 144). Sadly, this is often a designed choice of organizations to selectively listen, edit what is heard, upwardly report only what is favorable, and document compliments over complaints. This is also a clear example of an organization that is not able or willing to deal with unstructured input, which is another way to summarize rather than fully appreciate input that is offered.

Organizations may also work to silence inconvenient or problematic voices. We can see evidence of this in the Trump administration regarding the silencing of scientific experts. In 2018, the US Environmental Protection Agency (EPA) took moves to eliminate the science advisor's office. This role is meant to advise the administrator and to ensure the best science is used to inform environmental policies. Kathleen Rest, executive director of the Union of Concerned Scientists, wrote in a statement, "There's a disturbing pattern in the Trump administration of ignoring science, boxing out the expertise of career staff, and undermining the mission of agencies that are supposed to protect us." Michael Mikulka, who leads a union representing the EPA employees, told the *New York Times*, "Clearly, this is an attempt to silence voices . . . to kill career civil servants' input and scientific perspectives on rule-making" (Davenport, 2018a, para. 7). This is only one of the Trump administration's agencies where the elimination or diminishment of science and scientific advice has become a trend. There is no current chief scientist in the State Department and the Department of Agriculture, and both the Interior Department and the National Oceanic and Atmospheric Administration have disbanded climate science advisory committees. The Food and Drug Administration disbanded its Food Advisory Committee, which provided guidance on food safety. According to the *New York Times* (Davenport, 2018b), "government-funded scientists said in interviews that they were seeing signs that their work was being suppressed, and that they were leaving their government jobs to work in the private sector, or for other countries" (para. 7). In another troubling sign, "More than 1,000 members of the National Academy of Sciences signed a statement in April criticizing the Trump administration's decision to withdraw the United States from the Paris Agreement. 'The dismissal of scientific evidence in policy formulation has affected wide areas of the social, biological, environmental and physical sciences,' the statement said" (para. 16). At times organizational listening can be made impossible through overt actions taken to ensure that voice will not surface or that, when it does, it is muted or discounted.

ENCOURAGING SELF-CENSORSHIP

Stakeholders who hold few resources or little power are likely to self-censor, remain silent, and hold back negative news or critique. Research suggests that stakeholders who perceive that there is no receptive listener in organizations frequently remain silent. Further, stakeholders who fear retribution or other significant costs to exercising their voice will often choose to remain silent. Research (cf. Bisel, Messersmith, & Kelley, 2012) also suggests subordinates who show deference to and agree with their supervisors receive more favorable job performance ratings from supervisors and, in turn, tend to receive more pay and promotional opportunities than subordinates who do not. These dynamics frequently result in *self-censorship* and are well documented in scholarly research related to whistle-blowing, upward communication, and organizational dissent.

People generally dislike delivering bad news, critique, or negative feedback. This has been referred to as the mum effect in scholarly research. Researchers Matthew McGlone and Jennifer Batchelor (2003) argue that making a reference to something negative can be face threatening for the recipient and the communicator. In the context of the workplace, the *hierarchical mum effect* is described by Ryan Bisel and colleagues (2012) as "hierarchical constraint on upward information flow," which, they argue, is created through a culture of command structures in an organization. Command structures and related policies include ways of communicating; routines; rules; directions; and expectations for coordination, such as rules for using the chain of command, required reporting procedures, scripts that employees must follow, and meeting management processes. These structures often discourage some types of upward communication in organizations. Subordinates soften, omit, or equivocate when communicating negative news or views to superiors. Individuals who are conditioned to norms that limit candor will often block, omit, summarize, condense, selectively emphasize, and modify messages delivered up the chain of command so that they will come across "softer" or less threatening to those in powerful positions (examples of this were illustrated in the earlier examples of human resource personnel editing the input from employees about change programs).

According to Milliken, Morrison, and Hewlin (2003), "since people tend to be silent about bad news, positive information is likely to flow up organizational hierarchies much more readily than negative information" (p. 23). They cite the following example of Enron (see Case Box 2.1):

> A salient real-world example of these dynamics can be seen in the recent events at Enron. News reports suggest that many Enron employees had concerns about the firm's activities but were afraid to speak to their bosses about these concerns. According to the testimony of Sherron Watkins, a vice-president at the company, there was "a culture of intimidation at Enron where there was widespread knowledge of the company's shaky finances," [Oppel, 2002, para. 4] yet no one felt confident enough to raise these issues. (p. 3)

CASE BOX 2.1: THE STORY OF ENRON

The story of Enron Corporation is the story of a company that reached dramatic heights only to face a dizzying fall. Its collapse affected thousands of employees and shook Wall Street to its core. At Enron's peak, its shares were worth $90.75; when it declared bankruptcy on December 2, 2001, it was trading at $0.26. To this day, many wonder how such a powerful business, at the time one of the largest companies in the United States, disintegrated almost overnight and how it managed to fool the regulators with fake holdings and off-the-books accounting for so long.

Through a variety of shady business practices and unsustainable, overleveraged, and illegal actions, it was headed for catastrophe. A major player in the Enron scandal was Enron's accounting firm, Arthur Andersen LLP. As one of the five largest accounting firms in the United States at the time, Andersen had a reputation for high standards and quality risk management. However, despite Enron's poor accounting practices, Arthur Andersen offered its stamp of approval, for years signing off on the corporate reports, which was enough for investors and regulators alike. This game couldn't go on forever, however, and, by April 2001, many analysts started to question Enron's earnings and transparency.

Adapted from Segal, T. (2019, May 29). Enron scandal: The fall of a Wall Street darling. *Investopedia*. Retrieved from https://www.investopedia.com/updates/enron-scandal-summary/.

Numerous factors have been investigated to explain why employees and other knowledgeable stakeholders stay "mum" when observing risky activities, morally questionable decisions, dangerous practices, or impending doom. Promotion ambitions, trust in workplace, fear of retribution, poor supervisory relationships, and cultural norms within the organization have been pegged as major factors in explaining self-censoring and silence. Scholars who have examined whistle-blowing, dissent communication, upward feedback, and participation in solicited feedback sessions point to reactions such as the following:

- You don't want to hear what I have to say.
- You will punish me or withhold rewards if I say what I know.
- Our relationship will be damaged if I tell you the truth.
- People I rely on will distance themselves from me if I speak up.
- What I say will not matter since no one will take action.
- No one will listen to me because I am viewed as not having enough credibility, expertise, power, authority, or experience or because you think I'm annoying or a problem person.
- You will disregard what I say because I threaten your job security or power.

Milliken and colleagues (2012) illustrate these perspectives in their interview study about why employees fail to speak up in their organizations. Interviewees reported the following examples of self-censoring:

> "When there are holes in the research process, we generally don't say anything to the directors of the projects." (male, not-for-profit organization)

> "If you question certain processes, they made it sound like you were complaining and not being constructive so you were pressured to just grin and bear it. I didn't like it at all. Was one of the contributing factors for leaving." (male, accounting firm)

> "Retention of employees was a major issue. Instead of facing the problems and looking for reasons why, my employer treated those who left as traitors. The company discouraged people to speak up. Solutions offered by employees were quieted by (sic) immediate supervisors." (male, accounting firm) (p. 11)

The most frequently cited reason for silence on these and other issues was the fear of being labeled or viewed negatively by others:

> "There is a general fear of being labeled a troublemaker or a complainer. The management does not want to get involved with sexual harassment issues. In

this kind of industry you can get labels very quickly, so I along with other women do not complain about the sexual harassment stuff. It is a hush, hush kind of a thing." (female, sales and trading)

"Because it is a consensus-oriented environment, your power comes from whether people see you as agreeable and easy to work with. Being a rebel is not embraced." (female, investment banking firm) (p. 13)

The same study identified the second most commonly expressed fear, that speaking up about problems or issues was dangerous because it could damage their relationships with people on whom they relied either for information or to get their jobs done. The third most common reason given for self-censoring was the expectation that nothing would be accomplished by speaking up: "It's not so much that I can't communicate than [it is] their inability to hear me. There are varying degrees of listening and hearing. If they are not hearing—how hard do you push?" (p. 13).

Others failed to speak up out of fear of retaliation: "We have to be careful about the battles we choose to fight. When you get in the doghouse, it's hard to get out. I've seen people get bad assignments and get treated as outcasts

"My last comment 'appeared' to be inviting feedback. Do not be fooled."

Andrew Toos, www.cartoonstock.com

when they are in the doghouse" (p. 14). Others reported being signaled in no uncertain terms that their perspectives and views were unwelcome:

> "When I tried to introduce some new ideas at a meeting . . . the senior managers looked at me as if I was crazy. They made me feel dumb for sharing my thoughts. I received unkind emails in response to my suggestions. The tone was really bad. Now, I take caution before I speak up. . . . I don't take the risk of receiving the bad response that I did when I shared my ideas with them." (male, not-for-profit organization) (p. 16)

Although, certainly, there are individual characteristics that drive people toward self-censorship (e.g., low self-esteem, low self-confidence, lower achieved status, and lack of expertise), the signals (implicit and explicit) that individuals read in their organizational environments about the level of receptivity to their voice weigh in very heavily in their determination as to whether to speak up.

Recent sexual misconduct scandals at Ohio State University and Michigan State University provide further examples of self-censoring that have been worsened by flawed organizational design. As reported in the *New York Times*, more than 100 former Ohio State University students have come forward with allegations that a team doctor and professor at the school committed sexual misconduct with them (Edmonson, 2018). Accusers of the Ohio State doctor allege that it was an open secret in the locker room that sexual abuse was ongoing and widespread:

> The pair of lawsuits collectively detail three separate episodes spanning two decades in which athletes spoke out about the doctor's conduct: The captain of the wrestling team complained to another doctor at the student health center; another wrestler complained to the head coach; and two wrestlers confronted the athletic director. . . . "There were many red flags that O.S.U. ignored," Mr. Estey [lawyer representing four former wrestlers] said, pointing to reports that athletes at the time complained about the doctor's misconduct. "By not taking any action at the time, O.S.U. exposed hundreds of kids to his abuse." (para. 18, 22)

At Michigan State University, a team doctor was accused and convicted of sexual abuse of Olympic athletes training at the university's facilities. In this case, a series of individuals who ignored signs of the ongoing abuse or did little or nothing to bring it to a halt have been disgraced, suspended, fired, and sued, and the USA Gymnastics recently filed for bankruptcy. According to a 2018 report (as cited in Meilhan & Close, 2018) of an investigation on the events leading up to the abuse and the aftermath, allegations were lodged in 2015 and reached the then Olympic Committee CEO, Scott Blackmun, and the then USOC Chief of Sports Performance, Alan Ashley. Following are excerpts from the article by Meilhan and Close (2018):

> Neither Blackmun nor Ashley "shared the information received from Mr. Penny [then CEO of USA Gymnastics] with others in the organization, and the USOC took no action between July 2015 and the date the *Indianapolis Star* published its account of Nassar's child sexual abuse in September 2016," the report said. "Specifically, after Mr. Penny advised Mr. Blackmun that USAG had received disturbing allegations about the gymnastics team doctor, Mr. Blackmun did not inform anyone else at the USOC of the allegations, including any member of the USOC Board of Directors or any member of the USOC SafeSport team. Mr. Ashley likewise took no action in response to the information that Mr. Penny had shared with him," according to the report. (para. 5, 6)

The report (as cited in Meilhan & Close, 2018) went on to detail the multiple failures of many organizations that "shunned, shamed, or disbelieved" (para. 14) survivors of the assaults. Quoting from the report, "Numerous institutions and individuals enabled his abuse and failed to stop him, including coaches at the club and elite level, trainers and medical professionals, administrators and coaches at Michigan State University ("MSU"), and officials at both United States of America Gymnastics ("USAG") and the United States Olympic Committee (the "USOC")" (para 15).

These and similar past scandals have frequently surrounded not only the specific wrongdoing by sexual predators in the employ of these institutions but also the silence of those who were responsible for supervising these individuals who either by willful ignorance or refusal to act on reports of abuse took no action (e.g., Joe Paterno in the Sandusky case at Pennsylvania State University). According to a *New York Times* article (Edmondson, 2018), Jamel Donnor, an author of a book on sports scandals, argues that, when colleges have successful athletic programs, "administrators are often more loath to act on allegations of wrongdoing for fear it will hurt the profile of the university—and by extension—opportunities to fund-raise" (para. 12).

Sadly, there are numerous cases, current and long past, of sexual misconduct abuses in organizations of various types, in all industries and sectors (e.g., government, higher education, religious organizations, corporations, and military), and they often follow a pattern of individual bad actors who are aided by systems that fail to attend or respond to signals of problems; attempt to silence victims through threat, bribe, or procedural delay; fail to report or document wrongdoing that could facilitate law enforcement action; conspire with law enforcement or other outside oversight agencies to slow walk investigations; and endeavor at all costs to prevent public disclosures. Often, these practices result in an exponential increase in the number of vic-

Table 2.1.   **Sexual Misconduct Predators and Their Organizations and Victims**

Predator	Organization(s)	Period of predation	Outcome/victims
Klein	Northwestern University	10 years	Resigned from university/29 victims
Nassar	Michigan State University United States Olympic Committee USA Gymnastics	26 years	Nassar was sentenced to 175 years in prison after he pleaded guilty to seven counts of sexual misconduct/ over 150 victims
Strauss	Ohio State University	20 years	Committed suicide/ more than 100 victims
Tyndall	University of Southern California	30 years	Retired/hundreds of victims
Sandusky	Penn State University Second Mile Charity	15–30 years	Convicted 45 counts/30 victims

tims. Only a handful of such cases are presented in table 2.1. Consider how an individual "bad actor explanation" could not possibly account for this much harm: decades of predation and, oftentimes, hundreds of victims, many of whom remained silent or shared their stories only with close family members. It seems quite clear that these organizations played a role in keeping hundreds of victims from going public or to legal authorities.

Investigations of high-profile cases have suggested organizational complicity in censoring and silencing victims, witnesses, and those who were in positions to investigate and take action. For example, in the Michigan State Olympic scandal, critics of the USOC have argued that deeply dysfunctional practices and culture are responsible for the abuse suffered by the Olympic athletes: "That power structure . . . renders athletes unwilling or unable to complain about issues including sex abuse, funding and training for fear of retribution" (Associated Press, 2018, para. 11). Senator Blumenthal of Connecticut said at a hearing at the Senate Commerce Committee, "monsters are often hiding in plain sight. And they are often aided and abetted by people who turn the other way, who fail to report or take action in the face of this criminal action" (Olympic Athletes and Abuse, 2018).

In the Pennsylvania State University sexual abuse case, the internal investigation report (Freeh Report) concluded that leaders of Penn State actively chose to conceal the abuse for fear of bad publicity. Quoting Kristen Lucas (2012), "As events unfolded, university leaders silenced concerns, discouraged lower ranks from communicating courageously, and fostered a cultural contagion of fear that permeated the university. The Freeh Report identifies a 'culture of reverence of the football program' and a 'president who discouraged discussion and dissent' as barriers to acting in the best interest of the young boys who were abused" (para. 5). Lucas identifies the Cassandras whose warnings were ignored in this case, which reflects a "pattern of silencing" (para. 5) in the university. She reminds us of the graduate assistant, Mike McQueary, who spoke up to head football coach Joe Paterno about an incident in the shower; the university police department's decision not to file a crime log entry following the first reported sexual abuse case; a janitor's decision not to report a witnessed rape for fear that the university would fire the entire janitorial staff; and athletic director Tim Curley and president Graham Spanier's email exchange determining not to involve outside authorities but, instead, to handle the situation internally.

FLAWED DESIGNS FOR LISTENING

Organizations often create channels for listening. These channels gather input, feedback, questions, criticisms, client/customer reviews, community perspectives, and reactions to proposals, among many other opportunities for listening. Some governmental organizations are mandated to take public comments before making decisions or enacting new policies or rules; private for-profit and nonprofit organizations will sometimes develop routines for wide consultation before making or executing decisions that will affect communities, available programs, or new products and services; and organizations of all types will engage with employees (and volunteers) about their satisfaction, commitment, suggestions, and concerns.

At times, methods and channels are well designed for the people and purposes involved and enable the organization to gain learning and understanding that can then be fed back into decision-making. However, too often these channels are poorly designed and fail to entice or enable stakeholders to provide candid, useful, and relevant input that can be used to identify issues, resolve problems, or inform decision-making within the organization.

In an extended study of a nursing team in a metropolitan hospital in Chicago, Surabhi Sahay (2017) aimed to better understand how this organization designed its efforts to gather input from nurses about a major organizational change. She found that the quality of input provided by stakeholders depended, in large part, on their level of comfort with (a) those who were collecting input and (b) the space where input was solicited as well as (c) how informed the stakeholders felt they were. Sahay found that nurses were reluctant to provide candid input after implementers' advertised zealously supportive announcements of the change. She cites one of the nurse respondents: "Those big meetings I don't think people would maybe say anything negative about during—Because it was a rah rah, you know?" (p. 89). Another nurse mentioned that she did not like to "meddle with other people's business or step on their feet, because it was too risky" (p. 89). So, for these nurses, invitations to provide input in the context of a rally-like gathering about the change presented real risks that caused them to hold back their own critiques. The design of input sessions coupled with promotional messaging about the change had serious implications for the quality and completeness of input that was provided. Stakeholders who are asked to provide their input often have serious questions about exactly how, when, where, why, and with whom they will provide it:

- Who was invited to provide their input?
- Why do you want my input?
- Can others hear what I'm saying, or is this private?
- Will my boss, coworkers, neighbors, or outsiders know my views? And can I know their views?
- Will I be listened to by high-level decision-makers or by lower-level personnel?
- Is this formal or just off the cuff?
- Will the decision-makers be arguing back against what I'm saying, questioning me, or just listening?
- Is this a one-time event or an ongoing conversation?
- Will I receive feedback from decision-makers about my ideas and concerns?

Stakeholders who are given opportunities to provide input are likely to weigh the features of the situation in which their ideas, feedback, and comments will be collected as heavily as they weigh the likelihood of desired response and the consequences for candor. In a context of external stakeholder listening, public forums provide an example of these dynamics. When citizens are asked for comments on the actions of community rule-making bodies (e.g., local, state, or even federal government; business and community coalitions; and regulatory agencies), listening design plays an important role. Ideally, such forums should encourage more than reporting and commenting; they should promote public deliberation:

> To deliberate, people have to talk face-to-face in order to examine a wide variety of perspectives and weigh the pros and cons of every option. That is what deliberation is—carefully weighing various approaches to an issue against what

is truly valuable. Deliberative dialogue is different from popular expression (sounding off), information gathering, and debate. (Mathews, 2016, p. 15)

Koschmann (2016) observed that stakeholder communication may require dialogue, which he defines as "a form of reciprocal conversation that enables the parties involved to have their voices heard and where multiple ideas can be shared" (p. 6). Heath and Isbell (2017) also center their discussion of listening in dialogue and argue that "dialogic listening is composed of sincerity, appreciation, embodied presence, and genuine curiosity" (p. 192). In sum, these authors suggest that organizational listening in public forums must involve authenticity, reciprocity, curiosity, and willingness to engage in deliberation.

Hero Images, Inc., Alamy Stock Photo

Unfortunately, these ideals are not always reached, and the psychology of groups involved in poorly designed listening sessions can produce toxic outcomes. Martin Carcasson (2018), the director for public deliberation at Colorado State University, argues that "people naturally seek out, highlight, distort, and remember the facts and examples that fit their perspective, and avoid, dismiss, distort, or forget those that do not" (p. 37). At times, the ways in which we design organizational listening activities, methods, and forums reinforce our worst nature and these dysfunctional habits of processing. As Carcasson (2018) notes,

> whether at the microphone at the city council, in the letters to our editors, on our posts on social media, or through chanting during a protest march, we predominately hear an extended collection of individual or likeminded opinions. Based on our human nature, those are likely simply a collection of rather biased views, rocketing past each other, leading to at best, no real engagement, and at worst, further polarization. (p. 39)

Carcasson (2016) asks, "How much listening or productive interaction occurs during citizen comment? At public hearings? Open houses? Online? How many genuine conversations are sparked where real learning occurs?" (p. 45). As communities work through difficult problems and decisions, there will come a point where convergent thinking is necessary so that those with different perspectives can come together on directions for action. The design of sessions to convene and listen require something different for these outcomes to occur:

> Public engagement of wicked problems needs to involve a broader range of stakeholders *interacting with each other* [italics added], not just given a chance to express their individual opinions. Most traditional forms of engagement primarily attract the usual suspects or those with already entrenched opinions, leaving the vast majority in the middle disengaged. Citizens rarely approach the microphone at council or board meetings or write letters to the editor to explain that they have sympathy for various approaches to the issue and are still trying to work through the implications and negotiate the tensions. Instead, the voices that are heard are those with a clear—but often simplistic and at times scripted by others—view of the matter. Again, alternative voices simply talk past each other without significant interaction or mutual understanding. (Carcasson, 2016, pp. 46–47)

Flawed designs for public forums are likely to create an environment where stakeholders are unmotivated and unwilling to participate and quality dialogue and deliberation are absent or nearly absent. Consider the municipal planning meeting example in Case Box 2.2.

A shift in thinking about public crowdsourcing for organizational decision-making appears necessary. We must begin "seeing people as a storehouse of capacities rather than only as needs. . . . Thinking of communities as the sum of the capacities of citizens has the potential to change the understanding of public participation from a right to an asset" (John McKnight as cited in Mathews, 2016, p. 8). Until we design organizations to listen, we will be left with shouting matches and vapid intake sessions that record random opinions of stakeholders.

CASE BOX 2.2: MUNICIPAL PLANNING FAILURE

The planning board of a small town in central New Jersey was beginning their ten-year master plan update, a process mandatory under New Jersey state law. The municipality contracted with a planning firm to conduct a visioning session, both to inform the public of a proposed change to the zoning code, and to collect feedback on potential forms of development. The proposed zoning code would extend an existing mixed-use zone over an adjacent block, currently zoned for light industry. The planners brought pictures of a range of development types and invited the public to place red or green stickers on the images to indicate their opposition or support for such a development within the township.

The content of the meeting should have been largely uncontroversial; no decisions were being made, and the affected area was very small. Yet, the climate was tense. From the public's perspective, this meeting represented a chance to fight an authoritative force descending on their sleepy little town. The planners had arrived to unleash the bulldozers and cranes of greedy developers with the intent of turning the municipality of just a few thousand people into "another Brooklyn," as one member of the public exclaimed. Another berated the change in zoning as an effort of the United Nations to spread communism and promulgate Agenda 21.

The extreme degree of paranoia was reflected in the surveys collected at the end of the meeting. Comments such as "leave our town alone," "keep it the way it is," and, "we don't want any more stores" were common and referred to an immense power perceived to be in the hands of the planners.

This example is not unique to New Jersey, and it highlights two key factors driving the cycle of contention: the hubris of planners in pushing grand visions of the future, and decades of strict land-use regulation. Both have played an essential role in encouraging a sense of fear and mistrust between planners and the public. Both must be addressed in the pursuit of a stronger city. (para. 4–6)

Reproduced from Maitland, A. (2017, November 6). The public hates planners but it doesn't have to be that way. *Strong Towns*. Retrieved from https://www.strongtowns.org/journal/2017/11/3/the-public-hates-planners-but-it-doesnt-have-to-be-that-way.

UNDERUTILIZATION OF ADVICE

Management and leadership scholars have identified common dynamics related to how those in power seek and use advice. For example, research demonstrates that organizational leaders weigh advice more heavily if it is costly to obtain and advisers are thought to be very experienced and knowledgeable (Tost, Gino, & Larrick, 2012). Research has demonstrated that those in power tend to be prone to overconfidence, risk taking, and an overestimation of the odds of positive outcomes in uncertain situations. These tendencies often militate against openness to advice and input. Although this may sound more like an individual character trait, power is generally something accrued through an organization's structure. Individuals in organizations are not powerful merely by virtue of personal charisma, intelligence, skills, and abilities. They accrue power through their position in a hierarchy and span of control of people and resources and the degree to which the organization views them as irreplaceable. For these reasons, the *hubris of leaders* is an organizational-level obstruction to listening.

In a field study of professionals and coworkers (See, Morrison, Rothman, & Soll, 2011), researchers found that individuals who regarded themselves as having power over resources and decisions in their organization tended to be viewed by coworkers as less inclined to take advice. The researchers speculated this may be due to enhanced confidence of those in powerful positions, but they also suggest another possibility. It may be that "occupying a high power role leads one to *feel the need to express confidence* and also the *need to refrain from taking advice* from others" [emphasis added] (p. 276). In other words, sometimes leaders may believe that they must project confidence by not seeking or taking advice. In a series of studies about power and taking advice, Tost and colleagues (2012) revealed tendencies for those in the highest power roles to discount both expert and novice advice. They found that competitiveness with experts played a role in leaders' dismissal of their advice. They concluded that

> although listening to advice is an effective way to form more accurate judgments, there is a potential social cost: Relying on others can be perceived as a sign of incompetence or uncertainty. . . . To combat the potential social costs of taking advice, organizations need to create cultures in which organizational members are encouraged to share information and leaders are rewarded for seeking and integrating the perspectives of others. (p. 63)

Leaders do not always get involved in every consequential organizational decision. Leaders in organizations of even modest size must delegate. Thus, organizations must determine where to locate strategic listening activities and, more importantly, accountability for the successful strategies for listening. As the Mayo Clinic example in chapter 1 illustrates well, it is quite possible for responsibility for the organization's listening to become so diffused throughout the organization that it simply is not managed and failures to listen are not systematically identified and remedied. *Diffusion of responsibility* for listening and listening-related strategies may lead to a chaotic approach to discerning what organizations should ignore or explore. In their book *Warnings*, Clarke and Eddy (2017) identify the problem of diffusion of responsibility wherein it is unclear whose job it is to detect, evaluate, and decide to act on warnings. They refer to the central question of Who owns this?, which haunts some organizations. In a similar dynamic as the mum effect, few people in organizations want to own an impending disaster. They argue that this creates a "bystander effect, wherein observers of the problem feel no responsibility to act. Increasingly, complex issues are multidisciplinary, making it unclear where the responsibility lies. New complex problems or 'issues on the seams' are more likely to produce ambiguity about who is in charge of dealing with them" (pp. 176–177).

CONCLUSION

This chapter has provided an overview of four major categories of obstructions to organizational listening. Although we can certainly identify numerous individual, group, and organizational actions and beliefs that can get in the way of strategic listening, the four categories reviewed here account for a significant portion of poor listening. When organizations are designed in ways that discourage critique, counter viewpoints, negative feedback, and red-flag warnings from being channeled to those in power; individuals are signaled to remain silent, lest they pay consequences for upwardly raising concerns; systems for listening fail to consider the perspectives of those whose input is being sought; and leaders are not open to being questioned, doubted, and provided with contrary advice, listening is likely to be flawed or absent.

REFERENCES

Associated Press. (2018, July 24). Senators take USOC, USA Gymnastics, Michigan State to task over sex-abuse scandal. *ESPN*. Retrieved from http://www.espn.com/olympics/story/_/id/24185965/senators-take-us-olympic-committee-usa-gymnastics-michigan-state-university-task-sex-abuse-scandals)

Bisel, R. S., Messersmith, A. S., & Kelley, K. M. (2012). Supervisor-subordinate communication: Hierarchical mum effect meets organizational learning. *International Journal of Business Communication*, *49*(2), 128–147.

Carcasson, M. (2016). Tackling wicked problems through deliberative engagement. *National Civic Review*, *105*(1), 44–47. Retrieved from https://onlinelibrary.wiley.com/doi/epdf/10.1002/ncr.21258

Carcasson, M. (2018). Why process matters: Democracy and human nature. *National Civic Review*, *107*(1), 36–39.

Clarke, R. A., & Eddy, R. P. (2017). *Warnings: Finding Cassandras to stop catastrophes*. New York, NY: HarperCollins.

Davenport, C. (2018a, September 27). E.P.A. to eliminate office that advises agency chief on science. *New York Times*. Retrieved from https://www.nytimes.com/2018/09/27/climate/epa-science-adviser.html

Davenport, C. (2018b, June 9). In the Trump administration, science is unwelcome. So is advice. *New York Times*. Retrieved from https://www.nytimes.com/2018/06/09/climate/trump-administration-science.html

Edmondson, C. (2018, July 20). More than 100 former Ohio State students allege sexual misconduct. *New York Times*. Retrieved from https://www.nytimes.com/2018/07/20/us/politics/sexual-misconduct-ohio-state.html

Heath, R. G., & Isbell, M. G. (2017). *Interorganizational collaboration: Complexity, ethics, and communication*. Long Grove, IL: Waveland Press.

Koschmann, M. A. (2016). A communication perspective on organisational stakeholder relationships: Discursivity, relationality, and materiality. *Communication Research and Practice*, *2*(3), 407–431.

Lewis, L. K., & Russ, T. L. (2012). Soliciting and using input during organizational change initiatives: What are practitioners doing? *Management Communication Quarterly*, *26*(2), 267–294.

Lucas, K. (2012, July 13). Scholar takeaways: Kristen Lucas comments on "Penn State leaders disregarded victims, 'empowered' Sandusky, review finds." *Organizational Communication in the News*. Retrieved from https://orgcominthenews.com/2012/07/13/penn-state-leaders-disregarded-victims-empowered-sandusky-review-finds/

Maitland, A. (2017, November 6). The public hates planners but it doesn't have to be that way. *Strong Towns*. Retrieved from https://www.strongtowns.org/journal/2017/11/3/the-public-hates-planners-but-it-doesnt-have-to-be-that-way

Mathews, D. (2016). Can public life be regenerated? A Cousins Research Group report on citizens and democracy. *Kettering*. Retrieved from https://www.kettering.org/sites/default/files/product-downloads/CRG%20Can%20Public%20Life_FINAL_Digital%205-11-16.pdf

McGlone, M. S., & Batchelor, J. A. (2003). Looking out for number one: Euphemism and face. *Journal of Communication*, *53*(2), 251–264.

Meilhan, P., & Close, D. (2018, December 10). USOC, USA Gymnastics officials enabled Nassar's abuse of athletes, investigation reveals. *CNN*. Retrieved from https://www.cnn.com/2018/12/10/us/us-olympic-committee-report-findings-firing/index.html

Milliken, F. J., Morrison, E. W., & Hewlin, P. F. (2003). An exploratory study of employee silence: Issues that employees don't communicate upward and why. http://homepages.se.edu/cvonbergen/files/2012/12/AN-EXPLORATORY-STUDY-OF-EMPLOYEE-SILENCE_IISSUES-THAT-EMPLOYEES-DONT-COMMUNICATE-UPWARD-AND-WHY.pdf

Olympic Athletes and Abuse. (2018, October 3). Richard Blumenthal transcript. Retrieved from https://www.c-span.org/video/?452353-1/usa-olympic-officials-testify-sexual-abuse-prevention

Oppel, R. A., Jr. (2002, February 15). Enron official says many knew about shaky company finances. *New York Times*. Retrieved from https://www.nytimes.com/2002/02/15/business/enron-s-many-strands-overview-enron-official-says-many-knew-about-shaky-company.html

Sahay, S. (2017). Communicative designs for input solicitation during organizational change: Implications for providers' communicative perceptions and decisions. (Unpublished doctoral dissertation). Rutgers, New Brunswick, New Jersey. Retrieved from https://rucore.libraries.rutgers.edu/rutgers-lib/55677/PDF/1/play/

See, K. E., Morrison, E. W., Rothman, N. B., & Soll, J. B. (2011). The detrimental effects of power on confidence, advice taking, and accuracy. *Organizational Behavior and Human Decision Processes*, *116*(2), 272–285.

Segal, T. (2019, May 29). Enron scandal: The fall of a Wall Street darling. *Investopedia*. Retrieved from https://www.investopedia.com/updates/enron-scandal-summary/

Tost, L. P., Gino, F., & Larrick, R. P. (2012). Power, competitiveness, and advice taking: Why the powerful don't listen. *Organizational Behavior and Human Decision Processes*, *117*(1), 53–65.

FURTHER READING

National Coalition for Dialogue and Deliberation: http://ncdd.org/
International Listening Association: http://www.listen.org/
International Journal of Listening: https://www.tandfonline.com/loi/hijl20
Center for Public Deliberation: https://cpd.colostate.edu/

Chapter Three

Important Contexts
for Listening in Organizations

There are numerous contexts in which listening takes on special importance and requires a nuanced approach and skills. This chapter will highlight seven contexts for listening: frontline interactions, interactions with "non-friendlies," cross-boundary relationships, organizational change, employee entry and exit, reports of misconduct and toxic emotions, and encountering diversity. The focus in this chapter is to draw attention to the ways in which the design of organizations' strategies and behaviors in these contexts creates blockages to quality listening and necessitates nuance in achieving strong listening.

FRONTLINE INTERACTIONS

Organizations have many points of contact with their clients/customers. These stakeholders are typically the focus of organizational attention. Front-line interactions are those in which the organization's representatives have direct contact, often face-to-face, with these stakeholders. Examples include retail and other sales encounters, service provision, help desks, call centers, complaint desks and lines, product delivery, client meetings, and myriads more. These frontline interactions serve many important functions for the organizations, including opportunities to listen. Clearly, these interactions often embody the main business of many organizations as they deliver goods and services to their clients/customers and provide opportunities to learn these stakeholders' needs, opinions, concerns, and levels of satisfaction. Further, these interactions are opportunities for organizations to form impressions and a reputation, as well as to recover from poor performance in the eyes of their customers/clients. We should first consider some concerning trends about the employees who are the "front door" of many organizations:

- Many frontline customer/client service employees are among the least well paid in the organization and often have limited or no access to benefits, ongoing training, and career development.
- Many frontline customer/client service employees are working part-time jobs and may have a loose sense of connection to the organization, leading to high rates of turnover at the front line, which further deteriorates the sense of professionalism and advancement at the front of organizations.
- Frontline customer/client service employees often have very rule-bound jobs that rarely enable them to make judgment calls and policy exceptions or create solutions to problems.
- Frontline customer/client service employees are rarely incentivized by the organization to provide excellent service, although some employees may receive incentives directly from customers (e.g., tips).
- Frontline customer/client service employees often are well positioned to observe how customers, patrons, users, and clients judge the organization, which criteria matter most to them, and what areas of service and qualities of products are most valued.
- Frontline customer/client service employees are rarely incentivized to report what they've learned about customers, patrons, users, and clients or provided clear channels to do so.

Low-wage jobs with few benefits are less likely to build loyalty, engagement, commitment, and autonomy. Low status, in turn, can make these employees invisible to higher-level decision-makers. Their opinions, observations, and intelligence about frontline matters are often overlooked or superseded by those in higher-paid, full-time positions. In short, managers often tend not to devote a lot of time listening to those lowest in the organizational hierarchy, regardless of what they may know.

Anthony Tjan, writing in *Harvard Business Review* (2012), argues, "It's the employees who are closest to serving and supporting the customer who get an unfiltered view of how customers interact with a product or service" (para. 4). As the author points out, who knows what dishes go unfinished at a restaurant? Bus boys and waitstaff. Who knows what clothing is tried on but not purchased? Dressing room attendants and sales floor employees. Despite the relative low status of many frontline employees, they often make useful observations of customers' behaviors; notice what pleases and annoys them; and come to understand how to manage their needs, desires, and disappoint-

Source: iStock

ments. And they also have likely generated some ideas about how to improve service, products, and organizational responses to these stakeholders.

Unfortunately, organizations are typically structured in a way to take these employees' input less seriously than their supervisors', who are further up the chain but have less immediate access to the customers/clients. Managers rarely consider either the important insights of frontline employees or their ideas about impactful changes in response to client/customer demands and needs. Communication channels with frontline employees typically emphasize downward information distribution and instruction, explanation of policies, training in scripts for how to deal with difficult customers, and the like. Organizations rarely create internal channels for frontline employees to upwardly share their impressions of clients/customers with leaders in the organization. Thus, the listening that is done in these interactions is often not channeled upward nor distributed to the departments and units in the organization that might make use of it to design better products and services or to improve customer/client experiences.

Further, the low status of many frontline employees also tends to be associated with lack of power to act in unique situations to benefit clients/customers. That is, organizations tend to follow a long-held bureaucratic management philosophy that enshrines the power to make exceptions that go against established policies, rules, and practices within upper levels of management. Those at the bottom of a hierarchy are expected to follow policies, rules, and established practices without applying any personal judgment. Oftentimes, these organizational structures lead to disabled listening at the front line.

In an online *Forbes* article, Lisa Barrington (2017) presents several scenarios that illustrate the empowerment problem at the front line. Can frontline employees substitute a menu item for the standard item, accept a returned item later than stated policy, or cancel an order after it has already been made?

> Each of these scenarios represents a recurrent service delivery failure. In each case, the representative wanted to help you but couldn't due to a policy, the 'system,' or the way they were trained. Were these frontline employees capable? Likely. Were they allowed to resolve a customer issue using just a little discretion? Unfortunately, no. (para. 4)

These examples reveal how overprogramming frontline responses to customers/clients can nearly ensure that listening will be limited and the perception of the organization's listening by frustrated stakeholders will be very negative.

Consider a very typical service interaction in the following example, which I personally experienced at a checkout purchasing a few items at a convenience store:

> I'd been waiting in a long line (of 15 or so customers) to get to a single checkout cashier (where there is capacity for three). I witnessed a lengthy back-and-forth between the cashier and a customer in line in front of me. The customer was trying to use the credit card system and getting repeated error messages, which the cashier was attempting to resolve in a patient and conscientious way. After several minutes, I leaned in and asked the cashier whether he could call another employee to assist the growing line. He replied, "My boss doesn't like to pay people, so we are always understaffed."

The "boss" was apparently not onsite. This employee, frustrated by what I would guess were repeated attempts to point out that they needed at least two cashiers during busy times, complained to the customer about the poor management. I'm sure most people reading this book have had similar encounters with frustrated frontline employees put in impossible situations who chose to respond to suggestions, complaints, and concerns by commiserating with the customer in front of them and disparaging their boss and company. A compounding problem with such interactions is that, as a customer, I felt no motivation to share my views with this employee because I could clearly see he already agreed with me and he was completely disempowered to influence his boss. Even if I had asked him to pass along my concern to his boss, it is very unlikely he would have done so if this was the daily reality of this store.

Those hopeless to have influence will likely not invest in an attempt. This is another example of how poor listening is sometimes designed into hierarchies and employee roles.

An added reason for managers to devote time to listening to frontline employees is that tending to their concerns, interests, and needs will likely improve the commitment that these employees bring to their positions. The reputation-building capacity of receptionists, waitstaffs, direct service providers, and delivery personnel is quite powerful. Sending out angry, disengaged, demoralized, disempowered, and ignored employees to meet the clients/customers of an organization is risky, at best, and potentially disastrous. A current example reported in *Bloomberg* (Boyle, 2018) is instructive here. According to *Bloomberg*, Walmart, the nation's largest private employer, asked its hourly workers to complete a survey rating potential incentives and perks that could be used to lure and retain employees. They were asked to rate on a 1 to 5 scale from "I don't care about this" to "That would be awesome!" The incentives included in the survey were quite appealing (e.g., childcare, tutoring, pet care, gym memberships, access to paid time off, gift cards, and transportation assistance). On the face of it, this appears to be a great way to listen to employees' needs and desires and then tune the organization to better address them. However, Walmart's spokesperson, Justin Rushing, seemed to negate all that strategic listening with his claim that "We're always listening to feedback from our associates on how to improve our offering and experience. . . . While the results of this poll are insightful, we don't currently have plans to implement anything based on the results" (para. 3). This is a clear case of faux listening that almost certainly resulted in a dip in motivation and commitment by the employees, whose expectations and perceptions of their employer were raised only to be nearly immediately dashed.

INTERACTION WITH "NONFRIENDLIES"

Communication with stakeholders who hold oppositional views against an organization is difficult in the best of circumstances. Nearly all organizations face stakeholders and groups of stakeholders who for a variety of reasons are antagonistic. Such stakeholders may include competitors, critics, protestors, or groups of stakeholders who feel that their own stakes have been harmed or discounted by the organization. This category of nonfriendlies may use a variety of tactics to garner the attention and concessions of leaders in organizations. Tactics could include letters sent to the organization; organized boycotts or other protests; social media campaigns or viral hashtags that demean, complain, or raise issue with an organization's actions; publication of op-eds or other unfavorable public opinions of the organization; pressure campaigns directly targeting the decision-makers, including union negotiations, work slowdowns, or strikes; and pricing wars by competitors.

To suggest that interactions with these sorts of stakeholders is challenging is indeed an understatement. Listening in the context of antagonistic relationships is always difficult. Common dynamics during interpersonal conflicts include

- defensiveness and power plays,
- hostility and emotion,
- misattribution,
- escalation, and
- withdrawal.

These dynamics can play out on either the interpersonal level (e.g., two CEOs in competing companies or union and human resource representatives during negotiations) or the organizational level (e.g., competing social media campaigns or difficult partnerships). Largely, these sorts of antagonistic relationships are marked by low trust and a negative history. Add to these characteristics a triggering event or context that serves as a lightning rod for aggressive action or overreaction, and listening may be absent or highly dysfunctional. In a chapter in the book *Interorganizational Collaboration* by Heath and Isbell (2017), I recently contributed a perspective on the challenges of collaborating with "frenemies" (see Spotlight Box 3.1). I make observations in this short essay about the common situation of competitive and conflicted relationships in collaborative partnerships. Such relationships may occur in interdepartmental or interorganizational contexts. Where there has been damage done to relationships and trust is low, listening and collaborating become challenging.

In some cases, refusal to listen to antagonists becomes a strategy. A current example illustrates the complexity of these sorts of situations. In 2018, Nike developed a new media campaign celebrating Colin Kaepernick, the football player at the center of the NFL kneeling protests against police violence on African Americans. In the wake of the ad featuring Kaepernick, numerous protests of various types took place:

- Some colleges dropped Nike. The president of the College of the Ozarks said in an official statement, "In their new ad campaign, we believe Nike executives are promoting an attitude of division and disrespect toward America." He also said, "If Nike is ashamed of America, we are ashamed of them. We also believe that those who know what sacrifice is all about

SPOTLIGHT BOX 3.1:
COLLABORATING WITH "FRENEMIES"

We often find ourselves in situations [that require] that we work with others whom we may not always like or with whom we have serious disagreement. Sometimes, those disagreements are due to personality clashes, past bad behavior, or a sense of being outnegotiated or cheated in the past. We sometimes have to make deals with the devil or at least with our frenemies.

So how can one engage in collaboration with one's frenemies? This strikes me as an essential question to answer given that many, if not most, of the complex and intractable problems in our communities, nation, and world will require frenemies, if not enemies, to engage in collaboration. Much . . . work about collaboration seems to me to focus on assumptions of a willingness to engage in good-faith efforts to come together and contribute to a "third way" (rather than rigidly advocate for one's own side or compromise away bits and pieces of what one wants). This is typically described as a creative process that involves a set of communication skills, such as integrative behaviors, expression of concern for others, emphasis of joint goals, use of problem-solving structures, and conflict resolution skills. While positive and, certainly, possible in some settings, it is less likely and perhaps unrealistic in highly charged contexts with deeply entrenched beliefs and long-held grudges. In such contexts, commitment to the relational maintenance dimensions of collaboration, the time-consuming process of building or reestablishing lost trust, and fostering of commitment to a joint set of goals and singular vision of a future may not be possible—at least in the short term.

It seems an additional perspective on collaboration is needed to address less-than-ideal contexts in need of collaborative communication. Such a perspective needs to address negative history, low trust, scarce resources, power differences, and conflicted goals in a context of crisis, urgency, and high stakes. This worst-case scenario for collaboration is more common than our literature suggests but is likely the most important one. Examples abound, from a local dispute about policing, to our congressional discourses around a plethora of policies and law, to international and interethnic war and hatred. It is hard to overstate the critical need for development of communication tools and approaches that would equip collaborative partners in such circumstances.

Adapted from Heath, R. G., & Isbell, M. G. (2017). Communication oriented toward consensus. *Interorganizational collaboration: Complexity, ethics, and communication* (pp. 258–260). Long Grove, IL: Waveland Press.

Source: Richard Levine, Alamy Stock Photo

are more likely to be wearing a military uniform than an athletic uniform" (Nathan, 2018). Similar statements came out from leaders of Liberty University and Truett McConnell University.

- Tennessee State Senator Bo Watson called for a review of any state-funded college or university contract with Nike, stating that he and his constituents want to know what it's costing taxpayers to do business with Nike.
- The Mississippi public safety commissioner said the state agency would no longer be allowed to purchase Nike products.
- Calls for a nationwide customer boycott of Nike products with the hashtag #Nikeboycott prompted numerous social media posts, covered in media, of individuals burning their Nike shoes and cutting logos off of socks and other products.
- In a reaction that we might expect was anticipated by Nike, supporters of the Kaepernick-inspired protests rushed to purchase more Nike goods to support the company's ad campaign. The company's sales seemed to have peaked briefly as a result of the counterreaction to the boycott but returned to normal within a few days.

According to the *Wall Street Journal*'s analysis of the Nike case (Safdar, 2018), boycotts generate buzz and may force concessions from companies but tend not to have meaningful impact on sales. According to the article,

Brayden King, a Northwestern University professor of management who studied the impact of more than 140 boycotts from 1990 to 2005, stated, "Consumers aren't as consistent with their behaviors and beliefs as we think. . . . People who say they've boycotted a product might not be in the market for buying that product anyway" (para. 11–12). The fact of this trend makes it much less likely that organizations taking action like the one Nike took are less interested in listening to the critics in the moment than they are committed to a long-term strategy of courting a larger number of potential customers who align with the original action. For many cases of public fights with organizations, winning over larger numbers of stakeholders is made a higher priority—perhaps the only priority—over listening and responding to antagonists.

In another prominent example, Amazon has been the subject of negative press and public criticism about the oppressive work culture in the organization, with some for years comparing working conditions to a modern-day sweatshop. A *New York Times* article (Streitfeld & Kantor, 2015) reported employees' descriptions of Amazon as a "soulless, dystopian" (para. 3) work environment of long hours that demonstrated a lack of empathy for employees' health-related issues. At the time, Amazon CEO Jeff Bezos said the story "doesn't describe the Amazon I know" (para. 10). Three years later, after other major big box stores, such as Walmart and Target, have significantly raised their minimum wage, Amazon announced it would raise its wage to $15 an hour for all full-time, part-time, and seasonal workers. The wage raise comes after repeated public criticism by Senator Bernie Sanders, who blasted the company for paying its employees so little that they had to rely on government assistance to survive. Additionally, Amazon has had to deal with lawsuits, picketing, and dissent from other critics and stakeholders. Upon announcing the increase in minimum wage, Bezos said in a statement, "We listened to our critics, thought hard about what we wanted to do, and decided we want to lead. . . . We're excited about this change and encourage our competitors and other large employers to join us" (Snider & Weise, 2018, para. 5). According to Jay Carney, senior vice president of Amazon Global Corporate Affairs, Amazon is now positioning itself as a leader of the movement for a new US federal minimum wage. Clearly, Amazon has made the calculation to embrace the position of its critics in this regard, at least, and to champion their cause, all the while heralding their own act of listening. While it is doubtful that this move will silence critics, the company can now claim evidence of a grand gesture of responsiveness. Although I would not describe the Amazon case as an episode of quality or strategic listening, it does illustrate what often happens in the context of conflict with antagonists. Organizations either resist and deny or give in and label it "listening." Neither the Nike nor the Amazon case is an example of strategic listening designed to learn.

CROSS-BOUNDARY RELATIONSHIPS

Listening in the context of boundary crossings in organizations often presents unique challenges and dynamics. Dynamics in interprofessional, interdepartmental, and interorganizational relationships typically struggle with a number of challenges, all of which may make listening more difficult:

- Competing goals
- Turf concerns
- Uneven power and resources
- Clashes of expertise
- Unfamiliar jargon, practices, and protocols
- Alliances and rivalries within multiparty relationships
- Lack of trust and related unwillingness to share data, information, and analyses
- Unclear hierarchy and lack of decision rules or authority

When individuals representing different groups come together to interact with other group representatives, multiple complexities are introduced. In such relationships, it is possible, and frequently the case, that parties perceive themselves to have split identities and loyalties. Individuals who represent various "home" constituencies (whether it be a profession, department, unit, or whole organization) will often feel responsible to bring back "wins" and to represent the desires of their group. They will also often feel some loyalty to the joint work of the partnership and to accomplishing joint goals and mandates. The split loyalty often increases the difficulty of listening with empathy, curiosity, and genuine interest. In situations where there are key decisions that commit or divvy up resources, determine long-term plans, resolve conflicted alternatives to a course of action, or address urgent crises, the likelihood of the above-named challenges is much higher.

Some challenges arise when teams are formed by individuals who fall into some normative order of hierarchy. For example, consider teams of professors, staff, and students who represent their own constituencies on search committees or policy-making bodies; teams of nurses, doctors, and administrative staff representing their professional colleagues in a team to make recommendations surrounding an organizational change; or teams of engineers, public relations personnel, and sales personnel making determinations about safety issues with a new product. Each of these examples illustrates a team made up of representatives that normally fall along a hierarchical continuum, ranging from those who tend to have more clout, resource control, level of perceived expertise, and authority to those who have less. Jody Jahn and

Anne Black's (2017) study of high reliability organizations (HROs) provides important insights into these dynamics. HROs, such as wildland firefighting units, surgical teams, nuclear power plant personnel, and airline flight crews, operate in environments that are unpredictable and dynamic and often involve threats to personal safety and the safety of those served. Jahn and Black argue "that high reliability organizing depends on communication patterns and practices by which teams enable members to convey information to those best equipped to make decisions and incorporate lessons from mistakes and failures into ongoing activities" (p. 359). The authors also observe that these teams often operate in environments of strict hierarchies and that the nature of these relationships can become overly central during decision-making and other interactions. They argue that "in particular, it can be difficult for subordinates to share partial information and tentative conclusions, which are the types of information HROs depend on to catch problems while they are still small and manageable" (p. 359). These dynamics may play out in numerous interprofessional teams or joint decision-making contexts.

A key challenge in multiparty collaborations within or between organizations involves the building (or possibly rebuilding of) trust. "Trust is a central component of collaboration and consists of the belief that all participants will be honest, exhibit good faith efforts to honor commitments and will refrain from taking advantage" (Heath & Isbell, 2017, p. 84). Oftentimes, sets of individuals meeting across boundaries do not take time to assess, repair, and develop or rebuild trust. Trust is not a mere leap of faith or presuming goodwill on the part of others. Trust involves expectations that are set and honored; practices that are designed with fairness in mind and followed consistently; and candid conversations about how decisions will be made, stakes honored, and credit claimed or awarded. These are the conditions for strategic listening to take place.

ORGANIZATIONAL CHANGE

As I discussed in chapter 2, the process of soliciting input during organizational change often lacks sincerity, and, in some organizations, those charged with these tasks may submerge or discount much of what is heard. When an organization's stakes in a major change initiative are at serious risk, a number of potential listening failures are likely to result. Those tasked with gathering input may be strongly motivated to report up the chain only good news, solvable problems, and positive reactions. Certainly, these dynamics may be a result of a larger pattern of communication in the organization; however, some unique dynamics surrounding change programs may encourage these and other dysfunctional processes. Major organizational change is often marked by conflict, perceptions of threat or loss, high-risk investments, and intense scrutiny of outcomes, any or all of which may limit the quality and amount of deep listening.

In addition to the dynamics discussed in the previous chapter, we can also note the dysfunctional listening that may occur when organizational change is introduced or first considered. Recent research about what causes organizations to make decisions to introduce a specific change suggests that pressure to adopt a specific technology, practice, policy, or other change may be exerted through the communicative relationships in leadership networks. In a study of nonprofit organizations' adoption of websites, Andrew Flanagin (2000) found evidence that these organizations' self-perceptions of their status and leadership position in their field were positively correlated with decisions to adopt websites. Flanagin found that leaders felt pressure to stay on the leading edge. This study and others have demonstrated that the reasons for making decisions to change an organization and the specific change that is decided upon can be driven in part, or largely, by social pressure. In this context, listening may be dysfunctional when it is not processed through proper vetting, assessments, and full analysis of the appropriateness of self-applying other organizations' situations, capabilities, and resources and stakeholders' perspectives. Further, as leaders participate in networks of other organizations' leaders, they may introduce logics and ideas into internal discussions, regardless of whether they fit. Management scholars have long investigated the tendency of organizations to mimic one another's solutions to common problems.

Giving in to pressure in leadership networks is one of the reasons that management and organizational fads spread. Miller and Hartwick's (2002) article in *Harvard Business Review* notes some common tempting characteristics of management fads. They suggest that *management fads* are

- *simple*, using a few words or points to convey a fundamental idea;
- *prescriptive* and easy to misinterpret and misapply;
- *falsely encouraging*, with vague overpromising of results;
- *one size fits all*, with little qualification or contextualization;
- *easy to cut and paste* and thus tend to be surface-level changes;
- *in tune with the Zeitgeist*, highlighting some attention-grabbing current issue;
- *novel without being radical* and thus rarely change fundamentals; and
- *legitimized by current gurus*, who quickly lose star status once the ideas fade.

In the context of listening, organizational leaders who are influenced to introduce change programs because "everyone else is doing it" are likely not listening well nor asking good questions about the experiences, contexts, difficulties and challenges, and bad outcomes that others are having with those programs. Listening before making decisions is at least as critical as listening after making decisions. Asking critical questions, probing experiences of others, and gathering evidence of the met or unmet expectations of a change program are part of due diligence and involve strategic listening activities. Listening for only positive reviews, confirming information, and success stories that become the object of envy and desire is more akin to falling in love than a sober decision-making process.

Major organizational change often comes with an increase in internal and external scrutiny of outcomes and results. Leaders, particularly new leaders, are expected to bring change to organizations. Perhaps the most common measure of the success of a new leader is not how effective the organization is managed but, rather, what innovation has been brought into practice and positive results were reaped. Case Box 3.1 presents a case study of this sort of leadership syndrome. Leaders who are hell-bent on bringing change often fail to listen deeply and strategically and may discourage others in the organization from surfacing concerns, critiquing, and reality checking.

CASE BOX 3.1: LEADERS MAKING FAST CHANGE

[Greg was] hired into a large consumer goods company as the COO, and the presumptive successor to the CEO, who planned to retire in 24 months.

Greg rolled up his sleeves and worked harder than he ever had, pushing the organization and himself. To be responsive, he studied each presentation deck and answered each email right away. To be accessible, he said yes to each meeting and one-on-one drop-in. All of this took time, but he wanted to do everything possible to prove to the board—and to others in the company who had been passed over—that he was the right choice to be the next CEO.

His projects redesigned the supply chain for significant cost and time savings, created a new structure to quicken decision-making and increase flexibility, and improved the new-product process. Managers grumbled, and the CEO wasn't as enthusiastic as he should have been, but Greg assumed these were consequences of the inevitable resistance to change. What mattered was that people were following his plan and responding to his direction, and the results were good.

To make sure he was being clear, Greg had a habit of using a sort of double-barreled communication approach, following up each request with a here's-what-I-mean explanation. And it worked: Subordinates listened, nodded, and rarely pushed back.

At his 16-month mark, as he prepared for his performance review, Greg wondered how big his bonus would be and when he'd be named CEO. Instead, he was told that the CEO would stay until the CFO developed the capabilities to succeed him, and Greg would be allowed to resign. The CEO acknowledged that Greg's changes had improved performance, but he hadn't won people's loyalty and his style was mismatched with the company's culture.

Greg learned the hard way that people at the top rarely fail because of strategic or operational problems; usually it's because they have poor self-awareness and mismanage relationships.

In going full throttle, Greg had misinterpreted the CEO's reactions and missed signals that direct reports saw his intensity as a way to get promoted rather than to help them or the company. His behavior blocked him from getting feedback and cost him the support necessary for success. And that double-barreled explanation technique backfired: People quickly learned that they didn't have to ask questions, give feedback, or even think creatively.

Reproduced from Ciampa, D. (2018, June 5). Why new leaders should be wary of quick wins. *Harvard Business Review*. https://hbr.org/2018/06/why-new-leaders-should-be-wary-of-quick-wins.

EMPLOYEE ENTRY AND EXIT

Opportunities to listen to employees are in abundance in organizations. Employees have daily, routine communication with supervisors, coworkers, managers, and personnel in departments related to support programs, such as training, development, and benefits administration. From the time of initial interviews through exit interviews, employees can provide innumerable insights into an organization's operations; flow of work; culture and climate experienced by employees; and quality of communication up, down, and across the organization. Previous chapters and sections of this book have already discussed obstructions to upward communication, self-censorship, and critique of leaders' initiatives and ideas that may go without consideration. This section will focus on the dynamics of listening during hiring and exit.

Listening that occurs during hiring is often first undertaken by someone who screens applicants (very often human resource professionals) and later by supervising managers or committees of interviewers. It is rare in large and complex organizations for only one person to be assigned all interviewing and listening tasks related to hiring; thus, this tends to be a collaborative activity. I've been involved in numerous hires over my career. In my first job, I was the initial screener for applicants in a human resource department. In the past few decades of my career in academics, I've been a member of countless search committees for hiring faculty and administrators. Across all of those experiences, I've rarely experienced a case in which all the interviewers "heard" the same thing from a candidate. It is extremely common for interviewers to understand and recall differently what an applicant has said. Part of the complexity of listening in committees or serial interviews is that there has been no prior agreement about what is being *listened for*. That is, even in organizations that carefully craft detailed interview questions to be asked, there is often scant discussion among interviewers about what they want to learn. And, where there are different ideas about what is to be learned, differences in what is heard will be more likely.

An online search of "listening in job interviews" produces a lengthy list of advice articles on how job candidates should attune their listening skills and apply them in interviews. Articles about how the interviewer needs to adjust his or her listening are uncommon. Candidate interviews are often a side activity for many who are involved. Supervisors and managers at various levels who sit in on interviews or are asked to meet candidates and assess their quality and fit for positions often are setting aside their daily workload to make room for meetings with candidates. Further, although those who do screening interviews may be more routinely involved in interviewing and have skills in doing so, they also often lack firsthand insight into the qualifications and expertise required for a position. In that context, some issues that frequently make interview listening difficult include

- standardization of interview questions, not always written by those who are asking them, puts interviewers into a rote mode that discourages active processing;
- limitations of time for interviews and pressures to get through many candidates discourage probing and follow-up; and
- differences in what different interviewers are trying to learn from interviews encourage vast differences in what is heard.

Exit interviews, which occur at the other end of an employee's tenure in an organization, provide additional listening opportunities. Typically offered to employees who voluntarily quit, exit interviews provide an opportunity for an organization to learn about employee frustrations, challenges to retention, and lapses in training and development. However, too often, both the person doing the exit interview and the person departing the organization have strong motivations to avoid significant revelations. The departing employee can rightfully be fearful of reprisals in the form of poor references or of foreclosing opportunities for a rehire down the road. The human resource professional conducting the session may be reluctant to prompt disclosures of dicey situations or patterns of dysfunctions that will necessitate paperwork and follow-up. This combination may promote nondisclosure and failure to probe. Poor listening is nearly wired into such interactions.

Everett Spain and Boris Groysberg (2016) surveyed 188 executives and interviewed 32 senior leaders who represented 210 organizations in 33 industries, headquartered in more than 35 countries. They write about their review of practices in exit interviewing, "Some collect exit interview data but don't analyze it. Some analyze it but don't share it with the senior line leaders who can act on it. Only a few collect, analyze, and share the data and follow up with action" (para. 2). According to these authors, "most companies ignore the strategic value of exit interviews" (para. 10). These interviews, if they do occur, often become a lost opportunity to listen strategically and learn.

MISCONDUCT REPORTING AND TOXIC EMOTIONS

Another challenging listening context with employees surrounds the receiving of reports of individual or organizational misconduct. For decades, scholarly research has examined internal whistle-blowing and organizational dissent. Researchers' findings touch on many similar dynamics as those described in earlier chapters wherein those who have reported or considered reporting wrongdoing have self-censored or been ignored, disbelieved, or dismissed.

The #MeToo movement sprang up following public accusations of Harvey Weinstein's sexual assault and harassment. #MeToo spread virally in October 2017 as a hashtag used on social media in an attempt to demonstrate the widespread prevalence of sexual assault and harassment, especially in the workplace. It started as a call for people (women and men) who had been victimized to be heard. The phrase "Me too" was tweeted by Alyssa Milano around noon on October 15, 2017, and, by the end of the day, had been used more than 200,000 times (Sini, 2017). According to an article posted by CNN (Santiago & Criss, 2017), in less than 24 hours, 4.7 million people around the world had engaged in the "Me too" conversation on Facebook, with more than 12 million posts, comments, and reactions. According to Facebook, more than 45 percent of people in the United States are friends with someone who had posted a message with the words "Me too." It continues to this day as a means to make visible what has been silenced—the objections of individuals in the workplace to being violently attacked, personally humiliated and threatened, and professionally undermined. At its core, the #MeToo movement is a call for listening and responsive action.

The promotion of silence in cases of workplace sexual violence and harassment has been prevalent not only in organizations but also across entire professions and industries. The cases of Harvey Weinstein, Bill Cosby, Kevin Spacey, Charlie Rose, and Roger Ailes, among many others, illustrate tactics of bribing victims and witnesses into silence, retribution against accusers, and threats and actions to discredit those who report wrongdoing in the entertainment industry. For example, after the Weinstein accusations came to light, *The New Yorker* published an article by Ronan Farrow alleging that Weinstein hired private investigators to collect information about the women who had accused him of harassment or assault. Further, it is not uncommon for men accused of sexual misconduct to arrange or attempt to arrange legal deals that would guarantee silence in exchange for financial payoffs.

#MeToo allegations in government and corporate settings are also abundant, including senators (e.g., Al Franken), congressmen (e.g., John Conyers), candidates (e.g., Roy Moore), a Supreme Court nominee (Brett Kavanaugh), and a US president (Donald Trump) and recent accusers calling out executives and prominent employees at Amazon Studios, Fidelity Investments, CBS, Guess, American Media Inc., and Virgin. Higher education is not immune to the problems of sexual misconduct, including for students, faculty, staff, and administrators. In a recent article in the *Chronicle of Higher Education* (Gluckman, Read, Mangan, & Quilantan, 2017), the authors review a number of significant cases of sexual misconduct at the University of North Alabama, University of Wisconsin at Milwaukee, University of Arizona, University of California, University of Texas, and Dartmouth College. There appears to be no sector of our economy or organizational type that is immune to this type of misconduct.

As the review of sexual misconduct cases discussed in the previous chapter suggests, organizations must be designed in ways to ensure that concerns about internal misconduct are heard, reviewed, followed up, and acted upon. For the likely obvious reasons of avoiding accountability, preserving reputation, and discomfort in confronting ethical lapses, organizations are often resistant to taking such steps. However, the costs to stakeholders; victims; and ultimately, the organization itself can be dire if listening is taken lightly or insincerely. There are likely a number of barriers to listening to complaints of this nature. Some may wish to minimize "flirtation" or "joking around," rather than enforcing policies that prohibit creating hostile work environments. At other times, potential targets for reporting of sexual misconduct may certainly dread being on the receiving end of disturbing stories about individuals whom they otherwise respect and even admire. They may opt to encourage the victims to overlook bad behavior, excuse or forgive, or move to new assignments to avoid offenders. However, for some organizations, failure to rigorously pursue such misconduct reports may relate to the strategic decision to not know or acknowledge what is happening in the organization. Organizations with patterns of tolerance for sexual harassment and sexual assault may refuse to listen.

Some organizations have made significant efforts to set up specific and official procedures for reporting misconduct or expressing dissent. The US State Department's use of "dissent cables," established in 1971 as a response to concerns that dissenting opinions and constructive criticism were suppressed or ignored during the Vietnam War, provides an interesting example. Dissent channels are a messaging method for foreign service officers and other US citizens employed by the State Department to express constructive criticism of government policy. Under department regulations, diplomats who submit dissent cables are supposed to be protected from retaliation or reprisal. Since 1971, the dissent cables have been used slightly over 100 times, mostly by single employees. In an unprecedented case in 2017, approximately 1,000 foreign service officers and State Department employees used a dissent cable to protest President Trump's order to temporarily bar citizens from seven Muslim-majority countries. Despite the intention of dissent cables to be officially tolerated, several veteran diplomats noted that dissent was still risky. According to interviews by the *New York Times* (Gettleman, 2017) following the cable, senior diplomats said that, when it comes to a highly competitive and subjective process of selecting employees for ambassadorships, previous dissent could easily be used against a person. Some State Department officials refused to sign the letter because of the risks.

The Wells Fargo whistle-blowing events of 2016 provide an example illustrating how internal reports of unethical behavior are not always corrected. In fact, despite policies purporting to guarantee protection for internal whistle-blowers, this is not always the case. In 2016, Wells Fargo became embroiled in a massive scandal in which bank employees were encouraged to open credit card accounts for customers without their knowledge, leading to even larger systemic fraud. Whistle-blower Jessie Guitron lost her job as a result of working to raise warnings:

Guitron began working for Wells Fargo in 2008. Soon after, though, she realized they all faced a company-mandated quota to sign up new accounts. Some of her colleagues, she noticed, were promising to open free accounts for clients but signing them up for premium accounts which came with hefty fees. Customers were overdrawn, and their credit ruined.

"I kept complaining and complaining, and nothing ever gets done," Guitron says. "I was doing what my conscience was telling me to do. It's fraud. That's what it is."

Trying to stop that fraud put a target on her back. She was fired in 2010, she says, without warning. Unable to find a new job and believing she had been blackballed, Guitron filed a lawsuit claiming Wells Fargo fired her for speaking out against the fraudulent practices she witnessed. (CBS News, 2018, para. 4–6)

In a study by Stubben and Welch (2018), a proprietary data set from the world's largest provider of internal whistle-blowing systems, including ten years' worth of data for over 8,000 companies, was examined. The sample included a range of whistle-blowing topics, such as financial reporting, sexual harassment, and workplace safety. CNBC (Towey, 2018) summarized the findings, "According to the author's findings, whistleblowers play a key role in cleaning up a company's financial and corporate culture, and even help them achieve profitability goals. Firms that are more active users of internal hotline systems for compliance achieve a higher return on assets, the study found" (para. 4). However, as the CNBC article notes, the research also found that many companies ignore or mishandle internal compliance complaints and are frequently at a loss to cope with derogatory information that comes to light. One of the authors (Welch) was interviewed by CNBC and suggested that effective internal whistle-blowing programs can effectively limit lawsuits against companies. Welch is quoted as characterizing "companies without a whistleblowing culture as having a 'cockroach situation,' in which serious problems fester in the dark without being addressed. When those problems come to light, they become more damaging, and often spark a backlash against management" (Towey, 2018, para. 10).

Many of the issues, events, and behaviors that lead to dissent and disclosures of misconduct are accompanied by strong negative emotion. Grief, fear, resentment, anger, loss, and hostility can unfortunately be a part, even a major part, of what is experienced by those who dissent, disclose, and report. Peter Frost (2004) argues that "emotional toxicity is a byproduct of organizational life, and it is noxious. It drains vitality from individuals and from the whole organization. Unless it is identified and handled in healthy and constructive ways, it is a serious and often overlooked cause of organizational dysfunction and poor performance" (p. 112). Listening to individuals who are reporting difficult; damaging; and sometimes extremely harmful events, behavior, and activities often requires the handling of emotional toxicity. This aspect of organizational listening surrounding the report of wrongdoing further complicates listening.

ENCOUNTERING DIVERSITY

Most organizations are in some way multicultural, and nearly all are visibly or invisibly diverse. Organizational stakeholders (both internal and external) will differ in terms of gender, race, ethnicity, national origin, sexual identity, religion, economic class background, age, physical ability or disability, and physical and mental health. Engaging those whom we consider to be "others" can be complex as a result of the ways in which we have been socialized by families, schools, and communities as well as the historical, political, and cultural beliefs that inform our expectations and assumptions about those who are different from us. Potential issues in these encounters include

- stereotyping, prejudice, and discrimination—perceived and real;
- overt hostility and intolerance;
- sensitivities surrounding offensive terms and problematic inquiries;
- accommodation of needs (e.g., alternative foods, accessibility, religious observances, privacy, quiet space for persons with mental health disability, and braille signage);
- difficulties with accents, language, and cultural concept differences;
- difficulties interpreting nonverbal cues;
- variation in attitudes and interpretations of sexual or romantic overtures and comments on gender-appropriate dress, manner, or talk;
- misunderstandings of different standards of politeness (e.g., interruptions, overlapping talk, silence, order of speaking, and handshaking);
- misunderstandings and conflicts related to unfulfilled expectations;
- forced conformity to narrow standards; and
- willful or benign ignorance and misinterpretations surrounding dress; food preferences; religious restrictions and practices; forms of address; use of humor; socializing and drinking alcohol; personal disclosures; time and timeliness; emotional displays; and forwarding ideas, suggestions, and complaints.

This list alone demonstrates the high potential for listening to be complex. Even for those inclined to be sensitive, open-minded, multicultural, and collaborative, the differences among people and the inaccurate assumptions we make about meaning, intention, behavior, and emotions of one another can lead us into error very easily. Further, organizational culture and inflexibility and assumptions built into processes, structures, and methods of exchanging information can trigger the complexities noted above.

Useful definitions of *cultural and diversity sensitivity* include components of awareness; avoidance of judgment; and willingness to engage with authenticity, openness to learn, and willingness to resolve conflict. Strategic listening is both enhanced and challenged by organizational diversity. The more diverse organizations are, the more resources they have on hand to understand, interpret, and appreciate stakeholders with requests, unmet needs, and concerns. On the other hand, organizations whose workforce is widely diverse along multiple dimensions will need to learn to be flexible, appreciate the value of difference, and understand that extra steps may be required to engage in listening.

An example of the difficulties of being a good listener in a multicultural setting is provided by a description of a translation glossary tool that was created to help aid workers to listen better to Rohingya refugees (see Case Box 3.2). Rohingya is an oral language with no standardized written script, which has made translation difficult. The individual efforts, skills, and willingness of volunteer aid workers were not enough to surmount this listening challenge. The collaborative efforts of experts and a methodology for sharing knowledge across organizations were a necessary response to the complex intercultural interactions that were needed. Without an organizational response that enabled individual language experts to identify problems in communication, discover work-arounds in the language, and provide a shared database of these suggestions, the individual aid workers would have been far less effective in their communication. As some of the examples in this case illustrate, listening (even by very motivated and willing aid workers) can be made nearly impossible without shared processes and tools.

CASE BOX 3.2:
THE GLOSSARY TOOL TO MAKE LISTENING POSSIBLE

The word *haiz* means "menstruation" in Rohingya, but it isn't the term a young woman would use to describe her period. Instead, she might rely on the euphemism *gusol*, which means "to shower." That may seem a small detail, but it could mean the difference between a health worker obtaining an accurate medical history or deeply embarrassing a patient. It's one of 700 terms that will be available in an updated online glossary to help aid workers and interpreters to communicate with the one million Rohingya refugees they currently serve in Bangladesh's coastal region of Cox's Bazar.

In partnership with humanitarian aid groups responding to the crisis, the nonprofit Translators Without Borders has so far focused on translating "problem" terms related to water and sanitation, but the group is adding 500 words to the glossary this week to address emergency operations, disability, and gender. The list of terms is available online and via a downloadable app that functions offline to allow aid workers in the field to look up and listen to the words—each translated in the five languages. . . . In a city-sized refugee camp, misunderstandings and communication barriers slow aid delivery and can put lives at risk, especially if vulnerable people are missing out on vital information about health services or cyclone safety plans.

[For example], the glossary tackles the idea of confidentiality and privacy, for which there is no direct translation in Rohingya. And the concept of women-friendly spaces—the shelters dispersed throughout the camps where women are encouraged to relax, participate in discussions, and learn new skills—was also foreign and hard to communicate. The Bangla and Burmese equivalents didn't make sense to the Rohingya community, Rahim said. Instead, women started calling the spaces *garmens*, he explained. The word is a Chittagonian take on the word "garments," which the Rohingya community adopted since women sometimes sew in these spaces.

Adapted from Rogers, K. (2018, September 20). 700 words and expressions to help aid workers to communicate with Rohingya refugees. *Devex*. Retrieved from https://www.devex.com/news/700-words-and-expressions-to-help-aid-workers-communicate-with-rohingya-refugees-93470.

CONCLUSION

Although the seven difficult organizational contexts for strategic listening presented in this chapter are by no means an exhaustive set, they do provide insights into the challenges of listening when other complicating factors are present. Depending on the nature of the relationship; the content of what is being spoken and heard; the expectations of those who are listening and speaking; and the surrounding events, activities, and organizational and cultural expectations as well as the power dynamics involved, listening may become complex and challenging.

REFERENCES

Barrington, L. (2017, February 17). Empower your team and customers will keep coming. *Forbes*. Retrieved from https://www.forbes.com/sites/forbescoachescouncil/2017/02/17/empower-your-team-and-customers-will-keep-coming/

Boyle, M. (2018, September 21). Signing bonus? Pet care? Walmart surveys employees on perks. *Bloomberg*. Retrieved from https://www.bloomberg.com/news/articles/2018-09-21/walmart-mulls-perks-to-attract-new-hires-in-tight-labor-market

CBS News. (2018, August 3). Whistleblower: Wells Fargo fraud "could have been stopped." Retrieved from https://www.cbsnews.com/news/whistleblower-wells-fargo-fraud-could-have-been-stopped/

Ciampa, D. (2018, June 5). Why new leaders should be wary of quick wins. *Harvard Business Review*. Retrieved from https://hbr.org/2018/06/why-new-leaders-should-be-wary-of-quick-wins_

Flanagin, A. J. (2000). Social pressures on organizational website adoption. *Human Communication Research*, *26*(4), 618–646.

Frost, P. (2004). Handling toxic emotions: New challenges for leaders and their organization. *Organizational Dynamics*, *33*(2), 111–127.

Gettleman, J. (2017, January 31). State Depart. dissent cable on Trump's ban draws 1,000 signatures. *New York Times*. Retrieved from https://www.nytimes.com/2017/01/31/world/americas/state-dept-dissent-cable-trump-immigration-order.html

Gluckman, N., Read, B., Mangan, K., & Quilantan, B. (2017, November 13). Sexual harassment and assault in higher education: What's happened since Weinstein. *Chronicle of Higher Education*. Retrieved from https://www.chronicle.com/article/Sexual-HarassmentAssault/241757

Heath, R. G., & Isbell, M. G. (2017). Communication oriented toward consensus. *Interorganizational collaboration: Complexity, ethics, and communication* (pp. 258–260). Long Grove, IL: Waveland Press.

Jahn, J. L. S., & Black, A. E. (2017). A model of communicative and hierarchical foundations of high reliability organizing in wildland firefighting teams. *Management Communication Quarterly*, *31*(3), 356–379.

Miller, D., & Hartwick, J. (2002, October). Spotting management fads. *Harvard Business Review*. Retrieved from https://hbr.org/2002/10/spotting-management-fads

Nathan, A. (2018, September 5). College of the Ozarks to drop Nike from uniforms after Colin Kaepernick campaign. Retrieved from https://bleacherreport.com/articles/2794414-college-of-the-ozarks-to-drop-nike-from-uniforms-after-colin-kaepernick-campaign

Rogers, K. (2018, September 20). 700 words and expressions to help aid workers communicate with Rohingya refugees. *Devex*. Retrieved from https://www.devex.

com/news/700-words-and-expressions-to-help-aid-workers-communicate-with-rohingya-refugees-93470

Safdar, K. (2018, September 16). #NikeBoycott is over. Why retail activism rarely changes sales. *Wall Street Journal.* Retrieved from https://www.wsj.com/articles/nikeboycott-is-over-why-retail-activism-rarely-changes-sales-1537099200

Santiago, C., & Criss, D. (2017, October 17). An activist, a little girl, and the heartbreaking origin of "Me Too." *CNN.* Retrieved from https://www.cnn.com/2017/10/17/us/me-too-tarana-burke-origin-trnd/index.html

Sini, R. (2017, October 16). How "MeToo" is exposing the scale of sexual abuse. *BBC.* Retrieved from https://www.bbc.com/news/blogs-trending-41633857

Snider, M., & Weise, E. (2018, October 3). Amazon ups minimum wage to $15 hour for all full, part-time and seasonal employees. *USA Today.* Retrieved from https://www.usatoday.com/story/money/business/2018/10/02/amazon-minimum-wage-increase-15-all-its-employees/1495473002/

Spain, E., & Groysberg, B. (2016, April). Making exit interviews count. *Harvard Business Review.* Retrieved from https://hbr.org/2016/04/making-exit-interviews-count

Streitfeld, D., & Kantor, J. (2015, August 17). Jeff Bezos and Amazon employees join debate over its culture. *New York Times.* Retrieved from https://www.nytimes.com/2015/08/18/technology/amazon-bezos-workplace-management-practices.html

Stubben, S., & Welch, K. T. (2018). Evidence on the use and efficacy of internal whistleblowing systems. *SSRN.* http://dx.doi.org/10.2139/ssrn.3273589

Szep, J., & Spetalnick, M. (2017, November 21). U.S. diplomats accuse Tillerson of breaking child soldiers law. *Reuters.* Retrieved from https://www.reuters.com/article/us-usa-tillerson-childsoldiers/exclusive-state-dept-revolt-tillerson-accused-of-violating-u-s-law-on-child-soldiers-idUSKBN1DL0EA

Tjan, A. K. (2012, April 4). Listen to your frontline employees. *Harvard Business Review.* Retrieved from https://hbr.org/2012/04/listen-to-your-frontline-emplo.html

Towey, R. (2018, November 24). Whistleblowers ultimately help their companies perform better, a new study shows. *CNBC.* Retrieved from https://www.cnbc.com/2018/11/23/whistleblowers-ultimately-help-their-companies-perform-better-study.html

Chapter Four

Technology and Listening

Organizations are increasingly using technology to listen to their stakeholders, as examples in previous chapters illustrate. Newer technologies for organizational listening include those in the following list (Macnamara, 2016):

- Media monitoring applications and services
- Social media monitoring applications and services
- Text analysis and content analysis software programs
- E-democracy applications used to analyze online consultations
- Specialist sense-making software
- Argumentation software and systems

Many of these technologies are designed to facilitate the efficient interpretation of large volumes of submitted commentary. Other technologies are literally listening to us, even when we are unaware of who is accessing what we are saying. "Products such as Apple's Siri, Amazon Echo, Microsoft's Cortana, and Google Home . . . collect and record all sounds, even when not in use. The data provide unprecedented access to private information and bolster the specificity and scope of big data collection" (Jurkiewicz, 2018, p. S51). Although there are certainly powerful capacities with the use of modern communication and web-based technologies to enable sophisticated listening, it is less clear that the promise of these technologies is being fully or ethically realized in practice. In an expansive research project examining organizational listening, Macnamara (2016) summarizes some of what was learned about the use of technology in organizational listening: "Even social media, which were developed specifically for two-way interaction, are used by organizations primarily to disseminate their messages. Some organizations acknowledge that up to 95 per cent of their so-called communication is information distribution (i.e., speaking), while best cases have 60/40 speaking/listening ratio" (p. 235).

The adequacy of technologies to assist us in listening is highly related to the technical functionality design that enables certain processes to take place. Researchers Aldo De Moor and Mark Aakhus (2006) illustrate the challenges of using technologies to facilitate communication, specifically for argument and decision-making. They point out that a town hall meeting affords opportunities to assess the emotions and sincerity of various stakeholders but lacks the capacity to record the precise arguments that are made. On the other hand, they suggest that modern decision support software is highly capable of recording and organizing arguments made but makes it very difficult to evaluate personal motivations of participants. This side-by-side comparison illustrates that every mode or technology employed for listening comes with trade-offs in capacities.

This chapter draws attention to the use of communication technologies used to listen to organizational stakeholders in a variety of contexts. Clearly, use of technologies is on the rise in many organizational settings. Here, I provide some examples of technologies used to listen to different sets of stakeholders and discuss, at the end of the chapter, some general issues related to these types of listening activity.

LISTENING TO CLIENTS/CUSTOMERS

Use of technology to directly listen to clients/customers is now routine. Businesses use surveys and requests for feedback through websites, email, and smartphones. Call centers, email, and chat technologies are commonplace ways for clients/customers to pose questions, get help, and submit complaints. The chief advantages of these technology approaches to gathering client/customer feedback and resolving issues and concerns include timeliness, convenience, and curation. Businesses can gather data about a purchase or service interaction immediately after it has occurred, on a platform that is convenient to the client/customer, and in a way that can be immediately stored in a retrievable form for easy tracking.

Technology is also being used in the nonprofit sector to gather user satisfaction data. With support from the William and Flora Hewlett Foundation and the Bill and Melinda Gates Foundation, the Fund for Shared Insight created a tool called Listen4Good (L4G). Approximately 250 nonprofits are now piloting this simple online survey tool to understand how they can improve their direct services to homeless persons, food bank clients, persons with disabilities, and others. "These pilots are proving the importance of listening in fields where power imbalances between funders and beneficiaries can render silent the end user" (Twersky & Reichheld, 2019, para. 5). According to the Twersky and Reichheld article, an evaluation of the L4G tool found that, of organizations that implemented efforts to collect feedback, 63 percent are making changes to program offerings, 45 percent are making changes to their operations, and 31 percent are offering additional services.

Social media monitoring is an increasingly important trend in listening to clients/customers. Social media monitoring, also known as "social listening," includes a range of activities enabling organizations to listen to what is being said about them and, in some cases, to respond to those messages. Social listening tools allow organizations to collect and analyze a large set of relevant conversations in one place. Reports of social media activity can help organizations manage a building crisis, determine general sentiment related to their products and services, and discover new opportunities to promote their brand. Social media use is increasing, and the corresponding use of social media platforms and influencers as an important locus of organizational listening is also on the rise. An article in *Forbes* (Gingiss, 2019) reported on the 2019 social media marketing world conference in San Diego, where many top-level marketing experts advocated making social connections with followers and customers—especially featuring listening and responsiveness. The author summarizes some of the key arguments made by the experts:

- "[People] come to find out how companies they are evaluating treat their existing customers. And they come to see if companies are listening and responding to people in a genuine, human manner (para 6)."
- "[C]onsumers today expect that brands who have a social media marketing presence are also participants in the social conversation; that is, they are listening and responsive to customers' questions, complaints and compliments with human authenticity (para. 8)."
- "A company's brand narrative used to be determined by an advertising agency and the latest television jingle. Today, that narrative is being written and re-written every day by customers, prospects, the media and anyone else participating in the social media discussion. The experiences a company provides, both online and offline, cause customers to share on social media or ratings and review sites, and those stories significantly color other people's opinions of that brand (para 9)."

An impressive and sophisticated example of the use of modern technologies in listening to customers and public discourse in general is described in a 2016 *Fortune* article (Clancy, 2016) about MasterCard's Conversation Suite:

At the company's Purchase, N.Y., headquarters, product managers gaze at a 40-foot display that broadcasts feeds, visualizations, and performance metrics for more than 60 markets. When they want to dive deeper into the data, they retreat to Insights Alley, a clutch of casual lounges with 55-inch touch screens. And when they want to watch narratives unfold, they visit the Real-Time Marketing Lab, where eight more displays—nearly an entire wall's worth—highlight trending stories from services like NewsWhip's Spike and analysis from sources such as Prime Research. (para. 2)

The technology used through MasterCard's Conversation Suite enables an integrated media analysis system to constantly track over 6,000 keywords in twenty-six languages across tradition and social media globally, including content from Facebook, Twitter, YouTube, Pinterest, Tumblr, and Sina Weibo as well as traditional news sites (Macnamara, 2016). Certainly, the capacity of such a center to listen to a wide range of stakeholders in real time and to create retrievable data for custom analysis is quite impressive. The investment for such a system is equally significant and typically well beyond the reach of the typical organization.

While there are many methods for collecting customer feedback, there are significant challenges in figuring out how to analyze the input that is collected. According to an article in *MarketingTech* (Fanderl, 2017), many companies struggle with collecting, analyzing, and acting on feedback, which may leave companies tone-deaf to the voice of the customer (VoC). One challenge of the new technology used to collect customer input and feedback is that it is extremely easy to mindlessly follow a single or multiple metrics. What gets lost in metrics is the totality of a customer's journey with a company. The same article in *MarketingTech* argues that "[c]ustomer-experience metrics are everywhere, but relying on them isn't the same as truly hearing the voice of the customer. Rather, investing in an effective and complete system to measure the experience of the customer journey is the way to reap the rewards of customer feedback" (para. 18).

Mathew Bieber (2018) argues that VoC programs may be extremely effective in collecting input but are often not sophisticated in channeling that input into decisions. He cites customer experience expert Michael Hinshaw noting research that "only 29 percent of firms with VoC in place systematically incorporate insights about customer needs into their decision-making processes. And nearly three-fourths don't think that their VoC programs are effective at driving actions" (para. 3).

In the higher education sector, the "voice of the customer" is most often assessed through student ratings of instructors. Surveys of enrolled students are often used to measure the capabilities of instructors and quality of courses. Use of online surveys is a current standard of practice to collect students' ratings of instructors. Unfortunately, there is evidence that this shift to using technology to collect the data (over previous paper surveys) has produced unintended negative effects. An article in *Chronicle of Higher Education* (Falkoff, 2018) argues that student evaluations have become less reliable over the years because most institutions have switched to online systems. The article cites a 2016 survey of faculty members, conducted by the American Association of University Professors, which found that

- the rate at which students were filling out evaluations has gone down precipitously in the electronic age;
- the tone of their comments has started to resemble that of internet message boards, with more abuse and bullying; and
- students who were aware of some or all of their grades tended to be harder on faculty members in both written comments and numerical assessment. (para. 7)

Despite the lower typical response rate with online surveys, the same metrics of key comprehensive items (e.g., "rate the teaching effectiveness of this instructor" and "rate this course") are still being used in evaluation of instructors and play a role in their tenure and promotion decisions. These summary scores are easily calculated, stored, and compared across faculty and programs. Because of the ease of collecting and using these metrics, many have argued they are overly relied on to measure the totality of teaching quality. A faculty member's average score across courses for a period of time, as compared with the scores of other faculty in the same program or university, may come to hold disproportional importance in evaluating his or her skills in the classroom. Considering that the mean score may represent the attitudes, beliefs, and experience of as few as a third or less of their students, this is even more problematic. Further, although the student surveys collect qualitative data in the form of open-response comments, these comments are much more difficult to analyze, summarize, and compare across instructors, and, thus, they may be ignored or given short shrift.

As the higher education example suggests, the human side of customer service communication, whether by email, phone, or social media, can be quite taxing for the employees who monitor and receive commentary about their own performance through these channels. Macnamara's (2016) research into the reality of call center work illustrates these challenges well. After interviewing individuals who staff large government call centers in the United Kingdom, he concludes that

[w]hile listening to citizens is an important element of democratic participation and social equity, a practical reality is that some people are not nice. Customer

relations and call center staff report that some are rude, aggressive, nasty, and even abusive. . . . [O]rganizations need to have strategies in place to support and protect staff when they are addressed by unacceptable methods of public speaking. (p. 148)

It is very likely that technology-enhanced complaint communication is less civil than face-to-face encounters given the ability for the complainers to speak with more anonymity and to feel more uninhibited in the degree to which they follow norms of politeness and courtesy. Under such circumstances, listening may become more challenging.

LISTENING TO COMMUNITY MEMBERS

Listening tours, listening sessions, and town hall meetings are commonplace at all levels of government, from local parent-teacher organizations to state and federal political operations. Political and advocacy organizations, political candidates, and government officials frequently undertake some form of listening activity. The use of .gov sites or social media pages sponsored by governmental agencies or individuals in political office may be accessed by individual community members, who may leave their input, comment, or question. The degree to which individuals are heard and receive personalized responses in any of these channels is much harder to tell. Much of listening to community members may come down to taking a "pulse reading" of public opinion rather than parsing concerns and engaging in discussion or deep listening.

In some contexts, the focus on community listening has a very targeted purpose. In 2012, the American Red Cross launched the first social media–based operation devoted to humanitarian relief in Washington, DC. The Red Cross center is modeled on Dell's Social Media Listening Command Center. The center will help the Red Cross

- source additional information from affected areas during emergencies to better serve those who need help;
- spot trends and better anticipate the public's needs; and
- connect people with the resources they need, like food, water, shelter, or emotional support. (Occupational Health & Safety, 2012, para. 5)

In an online article about the center, Kenneth Corbin (2012) writes:

The facility . . . is equipped with three terminals and several wall-mounted screens designed to aggregate and display the conversations about emergencies that are taking place across Twitter, blogs and a bevy of other social media sites.

By charting that activity and displaying it in a variety of visualizations such as heat maps and discussions sorted by community, the Red Cross hopes to use to glean valuable information about victims' needs that is often in short supply in the critical early hours of a natural disaster. (para. 2, 3)

In 2014 and 2015, the Red Cross added new Digital Operations Centers in Texas and California. These centers are social media command centers that allow the Red Cross to monitor social conversations before and during disasters to help anticipate disaster needs and connect more people with resources during an emergency. Volunteers are trained to monitor key words and phrases during emergencies that will help the organization better pinpoint neighborhoods in need (Castro, 2014).

Although much community listening activity still takes place in face-to-face meetings and public events and through letters and phone calls, increasingly, we see a trend of investment in *civic technology*, which is

technologies that are deployed to enhance the relationship between people and government, by giving people more voice to participate in public decision making and/or to improve the delivery of services (usually by gov't) to people. These technologies can be developed by either non-profit organizations or for-profit companies, or even by government itself. (Donohue, 2017, para. 1)

The civic tech industry is growing. Technologies have been employed to provide open-source information sharing or to enable interaction between citizens and government. Luminate (n.d.), a global philanthropic organization focused specifically on "empowering people and institutions to work together to build just and fair societies" (para. 6), is actively working to fund innovations in civic tech. Luminate is working with both for-profit and nonprofit organizations with the intention to improve citizens' "ability to impact the decisions that affect their lives and also hold powerful people to account and create responsive institutions" (Mihailescu, 2018, para. 4). One of the beneficiaries of Luminate's funding is Phandeeyar, an organization in Myanmar that has brought together leaders from tech, government, civil society, and media for the Myanmar Digital Rights Forum. The forum drew significant attention to a set of critical issues related to online rights and freedoms and enabled participants to develop plans to address them.

The rise of smart cities may be on the verge of dramatically altering the level of technology used by government and other organizations to engage citizens. According to *TechRepublic* (Maddox, 2018), smart city technology spending reached $80 billion in 2016 and is expected to grow to $135 billion by 2021. Digital transformation of cities aims to transform environmental, financial, and social aspects of urban life. The *TechRepublic* article includes the following predictions by experts in the smart city movement:

- **Sameer Sharma** (global general manager of Intel IoT's new markets, smart cities, and intelligent transportation business): "There will be citizen impact; in general, citizens will be more engaged and will push city leaders for impact. Millennials and social media will play a more vocal role in the smart cities conversations and start influencing electability" (para. 6).
- **Charlene Marini** (vice president of strategy, IoT services group, Arm): "Smart cities look to improve revenue streams and citizen engagement. Expect drivers for smart cities to mature from just cost reductions (e.g., LED lights or better waste management) to better citizen engagement and more revenue streams, such as red light violation detection, Wi-Fi hotspots, 5G services, smart towers, and crime detection/analysis" (para. 12).
- **Ian Campbell** (CEO, OnScale): "We expect major US cities of the future to have the infrastructure to support cars, buildings, people, and things as they all communicate and interact with each other in real time, with very low latency" (para 14).
- **Ben Beinfeld** (public sector business development manager, WWT): "[Cities that succeed] will require a high level of innovating thinking and collaboration between different agencies, service providers, procurement/contracts offices, and community stakeholders" (para. 16).

There are numerous examples of the use of technologies in civic engagement on both a small and large scale. Martin Carcasson, a professor of Communication Studies at Colorado State University, who trains students to facilitate public meetings, makes an argument for the use of technology as an efficient and effective way to increase participation of and listening to community members. In an article in *Government Technology* (Stone, 2017), Carcasson critiques the time-honored tradition of citizens speaking at the microphone at public meetings: "In public meetings the person who walks up to that microphone is the one who thinks they have it right, the one who thinks they know the answer, and who therefore has the greatest bias" (para. 23). Carcasson makes an argument for the use of the iClicker (instant polling) technology, "'Imagine I put up a PowerPoint with 10 things and everyone with a clicker can indicate their top three, in rank order,' he said. 'If a bunch of people want to talk about No. 2 and only a few people want to talk about No. 7, then I can assign tables quickly and organize around that. It allows us to balance breadth versus depth by finding out what people really want to talk about'" (para. 25). This example serves to illustrate that technologies may be used to facilitate listening, rather than simply augmenting speech:

> Carcasson promotes the clicker as a way to get people working together, unlike other technologies that may enhance the volume of a public gathering, without really improving its quality. "We have lots of people talking, but very few people listening. Democracy requires us to interact, to actually listen to each other," he said. "Too often, technology just makes it easier for you to express your opinion, to 'get it out there.' And that can just create a lot of noise. Public processes cannot just be about input. They need to be public learning processes, where we get a more nuanced vision of the issues than we had at the beginning." (Stone, 2017, para. 29)

Other communities are making use of online meetings to engage more community members. According to the 2018 Public Engagement Report for the City of Lakewood, Colorado, the use of new technology for public engagement increases participation (Parker, 2018). Lakewood started the use of online public hearings in 2017. The planning commission holds its public hearings online as well as in person, allowing citizens to watch presentations, ask questions, and comment on cases via a website for two weeks before the public hearing in chambers. Different from neighboring communities that held online synchronous participation opportunities, Lakewood used technology platforms to enable different time and different place participation. The results were quite positive and remarkable (see Case Box 4.1).

CASE BOX 4.1: LAKEWOOD
PLANNING COMMISSION ONLINE PUBLIC HEARINGS

Participation in Lakewood Planning Commission public hearings is more than five times higher online than in person (based on views of the presentations). The additional participants online take advantage of the ability to choose the day and time that works for them, commenting throughout the day and over the course of two weeks.

The additional participants are demographically representative of the community as a whole in a way that is nearly impossible for in-person meetings. Focusing on using technology to increase representation appears to have significant promise when it is used to enable asynchronous and remote participation.

The hard lesson for all communities appears to be that we are not doing a good job of allowing public participation in our decision-making process. Weekly in-person hearings have extremely limited engagement potential. Communities that are serious about improving transparency and citizen engagement need to embrace technology. The same technological tools that we use in our business and personal lives can be used to ensure representative participation in government decision-making.

Fortunately, the answers are not difficult or complicated. Lakewood's solution has proven that technology can work within the existing hearing framework and without requiring additional staff. As early adopters of online hearings continue to add more options for participation, there will be an ever more obvious divide between those governments that prioritize citizen input and those that do not.

Reproduced from Parker, T. (2018, July 3). Public engagement: The future in 2 data points. *Strong Towns*. Retrieved from https://www.strongtowns.org/journal/2018/7/3/public-engagement-the-future-in-2-data-points

LISTENING TO EMPLOYEES

Artificial intelligence (AI) is playing a larger role in the management of human resources in organizations. AI makes use of a range of algorithms and machine learning tools that can rapidly take in data, identify complex patterns, and optimize and predict future behavior and trends. Human resource managers and other organizational leaders are making use of AI in decision support, natural language processing, gaming and simulations, knowledge management, and innovation generation. One increasingly common use of AI in human resource management is in the recruitment phase of attracting, screening, and interviewing potential employees. An article in *Financial Express* (Verma, 2019) describes the use of AI in combing through resumes and social media posts of applicants. According to a 2017 *CareerBuilder* survey (Salm, 2017), 70 percent of employers use social media to screen candidates before hiring, which is up significantly from 60 percent in 2016. Employers are reviewing LinkedIn profiles, Facebook pages, tweets on Twitter, and pics on Instagram and Pinterest. Also, AI tools are being used to "listen" to interviews to screen for top candidates:

> Bajaj Allianz General Insurance Company, for instance, is using an automated video interviewing solution, developed by Microsoft in partnership with Talview, to hire employees from multiple cities across the country. It also

uses Talview Behavioral Insights (TBI)—a job competency tool that leverages psycholinguisitics [*sic*] to analyse candidate response—to build behavioural profiles of candidates. These profiles enable hiring managers to find the right person for a job backed by data-driven insights. (Verma, 2019, para. 11)

Employee engagement is another domain for the use of technology and listening. Although engagement is a major focus of human resources professionals, according to the most recent Gallup *State of the Global Workplace* report, the current numbers are dismal: 85 percent of employees are either not engaged or actively disengaged at work (Werner, 2018, para. 8). Expenses related to recruitment, training, and undesired turnover are driving more interest in increasing employee engagement, and technology is increasingly being used by larger organizations to augment those efforts. There are many options for improving employee engagement. Human resource personnel use employee engagement software in efforts to solicit and track feedback, recognize employee achievements, and promote positive activity. According to the Werner (2018) article, some cutting-edge examples include the following:

Vibe is an algorithm that analyzes keywords and emojis sent among employees on Slack to gauge whether a team is feeling happy, stressed, disappointed, or irritated. Keen also provides a real-time snapshot of employee engagement by searching employees' anonymized emails to uncover word patterns and contextualize them as positive or negative emotions.

Other communication analysis AI tools, such as ADP Compass, Kanjoya, and Humu, give managers insights on employee morale—and offer subtle nudges on how they could boost it. (para. 11, 12)

In other contexts, technology is also being used to listen to employees in ways that protect them and their identities. For example, according to an article published by the Society for Human Resource Management (SHRM), new technologies, such as chatbots, are being used to help employees gain access to policies and procedures from anywhere, anytime (Nagele-Piazza, 2018). Chatbots listen to employees' questions and provide routine information. In some cases, employees report feeling more comfortable asking a chatbot about policies over a human being.

In addition to applications of technologies in recruitment, management, and engagement of employees, it is becoming more commonplace for organizations to create or enlist technology-aided channels for individuals to internally report wrongdoing. Whistle-blowing channels come in a variety of forms and range from low-tech (confidential hotlines or email addresses) to more high-tech websites or mobile apps. Organizations can subscribe to services to collect whistle-blowing complaints, enabling employees and others to internally report wrongdoing, rather than going public. Hello Ethics,

WhistleBlower Security, Red Flag Reporting, SAFE Hotline, and Got Ethics are a few examples of such services. Other apps, platforms, and websites have been set up for individuals to use to share concerns about organizational wrongdoing with one another to garner information and empathy and spread concerns about their own workplaces or communities. A number of such sites can be found on LeakDirectory (http://leakdirectory.org/index.php/Leak_Site_Directory). Say Something, Copwatch, and Agncy are a few examples of these sorts of organizations.

Use of these platforms is not without risk. Blind, a company providing a reporting platform, serves as an example of what can go wrong. Blind recently had a major breach of its data. According to a recent article in *TechCrunch* (Whittaker, 2019), Blind had developed into a major player in reporting services for corporate wrongdoing, including revelations of allegations of sexual harassment at Uber, which later blocked the app on its corporate network. The breach of data at Blind exposed many whistle-blowers who had used the app to communicate with others at their companies about a variety of wrongdoing:

> These aren't just users, but also employees of some of the largest companies in Silicon Valley, who post about sexual harassment in the workplace and discussing job offers and workplace culture. Many of those who signed up in the past month include senior executives at major tech companies but don't realize that their email address—which identifies them—could be sitting plain text in an exposed database. Some users sent anonymous, private messages, in some cases made serious allegations against their colleagues or their managers, while others expressed concern that their employers were monitoring their emails for Blind sign-up emails. (para. 17)

Clearly, use of whistleblowing and ethics reporting methods comes with some cautionary notes. Fear of discovery, retaliation, legal action, and alienation from coworkers or community members is reasonable in an environment where exposing powerful organizations and their leaders to embarrassing or legally troubling disclosures can make one a target.

Organizations and individuals who listen to whistle-blowing through these various platforms serve a variety of masters. For the services hired by companies to hear, anonymize, and report back to the leaders of a client company what has been claimed, the ethical line of serving a client and protecting the source of information is likely always in tension. Authors of a 2018 research study of more than 1 million anonymized records of internal reports made by employees of public US companies to NAVEX Global, the leading provider of whistle-blower hotline and incident management systems, conclude that whistle-blowers are crucial to keeping firms healthy and that functioning internal hotlines are of paramount importance to business goals, including profitability. They found that the more employees use internal whistle-blowing hotlines, the fewer lawsuits companies face and the less money firms pay out in settlements (Stubben & Welch, 2018). However, the authors also conclude that "Many companies continue to ignore—or misuse—whistleblower hotlines, and most don't know what to make of the information that is provided through them. Even when firms want to support whistleblowers, managers don't know what to make of reported level of internal reports" (para. 3). The authors note that some leaders consider the goal of these systems to end up with zero reports. However, others recognize that few or zero reports actually would indicate the system was poorly used and, thus, not providing benefit. The research suggests that high usage is a sign of a healthy organization with open communication, "After all, all large organizations face a large amount of common, unavoidable, and unobserved problems. Internal reporting systems simply make those problems visible to management" (para. 12).

Listening to employees as a means of performance evaluation and surveillance is another increasingly common use of technologies. Electronic tracking of productivity, recording of customer call centers, video monitoring of workplaces, electronic monitoring of keystrokes and company-owned devices are becoming more routine in more workplaces. Audio and video recording of meetings and disciplinary or evaluation sessions is also increasingly common. Privacy rights for employees are quite limited when they are on the clock, at the workplace, or using company equipment, and these new methods of surveillance are increasingly invasive. These topics will be taken up in chapter 5.

LISTENING TO REGULATORS, GOVERNMENT OVERSIGHT AGENCIES, AND FUNDERS

Most large organizations engage in some level of environmental scanning, which enables managers to forecast future opportunities, threats, and trends. A vast array of technologies and information management tools are available to organizations to invest in a range of scanning activities to draw in information and data as well as track dashboard indicators that are important to the organization's strategic planning. In a general sense, such activity can be thought of as listening. In the same sense that a physician listens to his or her patients' bodies through monitoring blood pressure, heart rate, and cholesterol levels, organizations can also design environmental monitors. However, just as there is a difference between a physician's lab results and body metrics on a patient and the patient's own reports of pain, problems, concerns, and health history, there is also a difference between routine monitoring of environmental signals and listening to important stakeholders in the organization's environment. Oftentimes, a deeper level of listening involves targeted use of technologies. Nonprofit organizations and academic researchers use websites and search tools to look for requests for proposals. Higher education institutions, companies, nonprofits, advocacy organizations, and local and state government use tracking tools and websites to monitor federal policy making and legislative agendas.

Employing lobbyists is one key methodology for keeping updated on governmental regulation and policies affecting organizations. Although we tend to associate lobbyists with influence attempts, another key part of their job is to listen to lawmakers and policy makers. According to the Center for Responsive Politics, there are currently nearly 12,000 lobbyists registered at the federal level. Technology is sometimes used by lobbyists in their work. For example, lobbyists working for an organization seeking permission for a controversial building project might host an online discussion forum about the project to listen to the public. Such an activity would provide the lobbyist with insights into both the issues and players who oppose the project in that community. Other tactics for monitoring opposition groups include monitoring of the internet to pick up the first warning signals of activist activity. Identification of influential people who are opposers might be followed with a strategy to discredit or silence their voices.

Highly regulated industries, such as pharmaceuticals, transportation, oil and gas, and financial services, have a strong need to stay informed about regulatory changes affecting their businesses. As the pace of innovation and particularly technology and internet-related change increases, regulatory rule making and lawmaking is hardly keeping pace, and new models of regulation are shifting to an iterative model (Eggers, Turley, & Kishnani, 2018). From e-cigarettes to self-driving cars to ride-hailing platforms to virtual currencies, the potential for regulatory complexity is high. Additional challenges arise due to conflicting regulations by level (i.e., local, state, federal, and international) and agency jurisdiction. This environment has led to a collaborative approach between industry, experts, and government in designing regulations that make sense. An article from *Deloitte Insights* in 2018 (Eggers et al., 2018) describes a new approach to traditional regulation:

> Adaptive approaches to regulation, on the other hand, rely more on trial and error and co-design of regulation and standards; they also have faster feedback loops. More rapid feedback loops allow regulators to evaluate policies against set standards, feeding inputs into revising regulations. Regulatory agencies have a number of tools to seek such feedback: setting up policy labs, creating regulatory sandboxes . . . crowdsourcing, policymaking, and providing representation

to industry in the governance process via self-regulatory and private standard-setting bodies. (Principles for regulating emerging technologies, para. 5)

As part of this approach, in some cases, soft law mechanisms (which enable standard setting without creating enforceable regulation) enable self-regulation. Such an approach involves crowdsourcing with stakeholders affected by new standards in practices. Collaborative models involving a good deal of listening among stakeholders, oftentimes through technology-enabled means, appear to be a major reinvention of the regulatory space.

KEY QUESTIONS ABOUT TECHNOLOGY AND LISTENING

New communication technologies of various kinds provide new opportunities and cautionary notes related to organizational listening. As with most tools, communication and information technologies may be used for good or ill purpose and may be used with varying degrees of appropriateness and success. As I review the ways in which organizations use technology to listen to various stakeholders, a handful of important questions come to mind. I discuss these key questions in the remainder of this chapter.

Is there a difference between collection and listening? The examples in this chapter make clear that "collection" is not the same as "listening." Powerful technologically supported methods to assist listening enable an impressive capability to amass huge amounts of data, information, commentary, input, and feedback from thousands or even millions of stakeholders on a daily or even minute-by-minute basis. As I discussed in chapter 1, collecting information and data is not the same as strategic listening. Massive amounts of data collection may create difficulties, such as information overload, inability to locate and extract relevant information when needed, and disorganization of information that needs to have context and be placed in the hands of the right decision-makers to make use of it. The mere possession of information, no matter its relevance, quality, or uniqueness, cannot be strategically used until it is summarized, interpreted, and put into some context of decision-making. In other words, information is not actionable unless there are other steps taken to make it so.

Although it is true that all information can be routinely, even mindlessly, collected without added steps to make it useful, strategic, and helpful in some decision context, this problem is especially true of information collected through powerful technologies. Because of the sheer capacity of many of the technologies discussed in this chapter to hardwire data and information collection routines into organizations, they are at greater risk of this dilemma. Listening, especially strategic listening, must involve reflection and response, rather than mere focus on accumulation of input. A danger of overemphasis on collection of input without also developing equally powerful tools and routines for analysis and consumption of input is that organizational leaders can become convinced that they are holding all the intelligence needed to assure themselves that they know what they need to know. This can lead to many of the ill-fated and dysfunctional practices discussed in the earlier chapters of this book.

Do technologies inhibit, distort, and prohibit strategic listening? We might easily assume that the use of a technology to aid our organizational listening can only add value and at worst would simply have a neutral impact. However, there are serious trade-offs for use of technology in organizational listening. Technology-aided listening may be costly and complex and can produce deleterious effects for stakeholders and organizations. Technologies may also introduce a new set of ethics issues. Sophisticated technology for monitoring multiple social media and news platforms can be costly itself, and added expenses of hiring trained information management professionals to design, monitor, curate, disseminate, and continually update the use of such technologies can be significant.

There are also potential costs associated with moving to more high-tech and low-touch modes of listening. Although there may be advantages to stakeholders and organizations that employ automated AI-assisted listening, such as speed, uniformity, and reduced risk of identification of speaker, there may also be a loss of trust building, personalization, customization, and benefits derived from human contact. We must be conscious of balancing efficiencies with qualities associated with high-touch interaction and more nuanced observations and capacity for dialogue. It is extremely efficient to enable multiple stakeholders to weigh in, provide commentary, and rate and rank preferences, among many other curatable input. However, the exchanges that occur in natural dialogue, back-and-forth discussion, and nuanced and complex storytelling that do not tend to lend themselves to automated, technology-aided listening may increasingly be lost to organizations.

Are there ethical issues raised by the use of technologies? Organizations will need to consider the ethical dilemmas related to increasing use of technologies in their listening strategies. There is likely a thin line between listening and "listening in." The temptation for organizations to automate eavesdropping on their employees, customers, and citizens because it is easy and affordable to do is problematic terrain. There are significant questions associated with continual listening, especially when done covertly. Who has rights to privacy? Can one opt out of being heard or overheard in some contexts? Who owns the data collected? Who may withdraw what has been heard? When something is recorded, can it be distributed at the will of the collector? Because technologies enable organizations to not only hear but to record and preserve what is said, added layers of ethical considerations are raised. These topics are addressed in more detail in chapter 5.

Is technologically aided listening creating distance or increasing connection? The use of technology to assist citizens in the midst of a natural disaster and discover their immediate unmet needs seems an excellent example of overcoming crisis through connecting people. However, using AI to analyze employment interviews to determine best candidates seems an example of technology substituting for the nuance and wisdom of human contact. At times, efficiencies and capacities of listening technologies may bring organizations closer to their stakeholders and enable connections that were difficult or impossible with traditional channels (e.g., paper surveys and person-to-person interaction), but we must be mindful that we may substitute some highly useful and important points of contact with dispassionate programs and algorithms if we overuse technology to do the work of listening. To use technologies in service of strategic listening, the trade-offs should be considered—both value added and value lost.

CONCLUSION

Listening with technology is in many ways a brave new world. The increasing capacity and affordability of services and technologies for listening to more and more speakers in a variety of online and offline contexts raise numerous questions about the utility of constant monitoring; the analysis of what is heard and collected; and the costs, trade-offs, and ethics of technology-aided listening. As with most any tool at the disposal of organizations, these capacities and technologies will need to be considered in the full context of needs, goals, and strategic intentions.

REFERENCES

Bieber, M. (2018, February 21). Your customers are speaking: Are you listening? *CMSWire*. Retrieved from https://www.cmswire.com/customer-experience/your-customers-are-speaking-are-you-listening/

Castro, B. (2014, April 8). Red Cross launches digital operations center. *NBCDFW. com*. Retrieved from https://www.nbcdfw.com/news/local/Red-Cross-Launches-Digital-Operations-Center-254471831.html

Clancy, H. (2016, January 29). MasterCard uses a command center to track its marketing spend. *Fortune*. Retrieved from http://fortune.com/2016/01/29/mastercard-data-analytics/

Corbin, K. (2012, March 8). Dell powers Red Cross social media command center. *CIO*. Retrieved from https://www.cio.com/article/2395627/dell-powers-red-cross-social-media-command-center.html

De Moor, A., & Aakhus, M. (2006). Argumentation support: From technologies to tools. *Communications of the ACM, 49*(3), 93–98.

Donohue, S. (2017, September 15). What exactly is civic tech? *Quora*. Retrieved from https://www.quora.com/What-exactly-is-civic-tech

Eggers, W. D., Turley, M., & Kishnani, P. (2018, June 19). The future of regulation: Principles for regulating emerging technologies. *Deloitte Insights*. Retrieved from https://www2.deloitte.com/insights/us/en/industry/public-sector/future-of-regulation/regulating-emerging-technology.html

Falkoff, M. (2018, April 25). Why we must stop relying on student ratings of teaching. *Chronicle of Higher Education*. Retrieved from https://www.chronicle.com/article/Why-We-Must-Stop-Relying-on/243213

Fanderl, H. (2017, October 13). Your customers are speaking—but are you really listening? *MarketingTech*. Retrieved from https://www.marketingtechnews.net/news/2017/oct/30/your-customers-are-speaking-are-you-really-listening/

Gingiss, D. (2019, April 2). 8 Quotes that define the state of social media today. *Forbes*. Retrieved from https://www.forbes.com/sites/dangingiss/2019/04/02/8-quotes-that-define-the-state-of-social-media-today/#41c737c86523

Jurkiewicz, C. L. (2018). Big data, big concerns: Ethics in the digital age. *Public Integrity, 20*(Suppl. 1), S46–S59.

Luminate. (n.d.). About us: How we make a difference. Retrieved from https://luminategroup.com/about

Maddox, T. (2018, December 19). Top smart city predictions for 2019. *TechRepublic*. Retrieved from https://www.techrepublic.com/article/top-smart-city-predictions-for-2019/

Macnamara, J. (2016). *Organizational listening: The missing essential in public communication*. New York, NY: Peter Lang Publishing.

Mihailescu, T. (2018, December 4). New philanthropic organization to boost civic tech as part of $60 million commitment in 2019. *Forbes*. Retrieved from https://www.forbes.com/sites/tudormihailescu/2018/12/04/newly-launched-philanthropic-organization-pledges-to-invest-60-million-in-civic-tech-in-2019/#1bf8741b3c3c

Nagele-Piazza, L. (2018, May 29). How can artificial intelligence work for HR? *SHRM*. Retrieved from https://www.shrm.org/resourcesandtools/legal-and-compliance/employment-law/pages/how-can-artificial-intelligence-work-for-hr.aspx

Occupational Health & Safety. (2012, March 11). Red Cross launches social media command center for disaster relief. Retrieved from https://ohsonline.com/Articles/2012/03/11/Red-Cross-Launches-Social-Media-Command-Center-for-Disaster-Relief.aspx

Parker, T. (2018, July 3). Public engagement: The future in 2 data points. *Strong Towns*. Retrieved from https://www.strongtowns.org/journal/2018/7/3/public-engagement-the-future-in-2-data-points

Salm, L. (2017, June 15). 70% of employers are snooping candidates' social media profiles. *CareerBuilder*. Retrieved from https://www.careerbuilder.com/advice/social-media-survey-2017

Stone, A. (2017, January 18). How technology is giving town hall meetings a modern twist. *Government Technology*. Retrieved from http://www.govtech.com/policy/How-Technology-Is-Giving-Town-Hall-Meetings-a-Modern-Twist.html

Stubben, S., & Welch, K. (2018, November 14). Research: Whistleblowers are a sign of healthy companies. *Harvard Business Review*. Retrieved from https://hbr.org/2018/11/research-whistleblowers-are-a-sign-of-healthy-companies

Twersky, F., & Reichheld, F. (2019, February 4). Why customer feedback tools are vital for nonprofits. *Harvard Business Review*. Retrieved from https://hbr.org/2019/02/why-customer-feedback-tools-are-vital-for-nonprofits

Verma, S. (2019, January 1). No more human resources: AI invades the workplace, bot becomes the new hiring manager. *Financial Express*. Retrieved from https://www.financialexpress.com/industry/technology/no-more-human-resources-ai-invades-the-workplace-bot-becomes-the-new-hiring-manager/1428503/

Werner, T. (2018, November 29). How AI can redesign the employee experience. *Forbes*. Retrieved from https://www.forbes.com/sites/insights-intelai/2018/11/29/how-ai-can-help-redesign-the-employee-experience/#727f40d24b34

Whittaker, Z. (2019). At Blind, a security lapse revealed private complaints from Silicon Valley employees. *TechCrunch*. Retrieved from https://techcrunch.com/2018/12/20/blind-anonymous-app-data-exposure/

ADDITIONAL RESOURCE

Civic Media Tools and Cases: https://elab.emerson.edu/projects/civic-media-project

Chapter Five

Dark Side of Organizational Listening

There is a dark side to organizational listening. The dark side of listening may cause harm to organizations, individuals, and organizational relationships. At times, organizational listening is covert and manipulative. At times, organizations foster a culture or philosophy that actively discourages authentic listening and casts doubt on the motives and authenticity of those who speak. In this chapter, I'll review examples of cynical and unethical organizational practices as well as the outcomes of toxic organizational cultures that turn listening dark.

EAVESDROPPING

Employee surveillance is a common practice in many organizations. Secret, or "mystery," shoppers; electronic tracking of productivity; recording of customer call centers; video monitoring of workplaces; and electronic monitoring of keystrokes and company-owned devices are becoming routine in more workplaces. Audio and video recording of meetings and disciplinary or evaluation sessions is also increasingly common. Privacy rights for employees are quite limited when they are on the clock, at the workplace, or using company equipment, and these new methods of surveillance are increasingly invasive. Paula Brantner, senior adviser at the employee rights group Workplace Fairness, suggests a number of uses of these devices: "Are the bathroom breaks too long? Are you chatting with co-workers? Wasting any time? These devices show if you're working at maximum efficiency" (Reed, 2018, para. 17).

An article in *Inc.* (Matyszczyk, 2018) reports on recent research about the degree of electronic surveillance of employees. The study asked more than 300 information technology (IT) professionals working in companies with more than 500 employees about what those companies are really doing behind the digital scenes. Here are some of the findings of this study:

- 98 percent of the IT professionals admitted that the companies do, indeed, monitor their employees' digital behavior.
- The IT professionals say that only 11 percent of employees are aware of just how deeply companies dig.
- 11 percent of employees have no idea that their companies spy on them at all.
- 87 percent of companies apparently track their employees' email.
- 70 percent of companies grab employees' whole web browser history.
- 41 percent of companies creep in on voice mails.
- 34 percent look through the peephole to observe LinkedIn and Facebook activity.
- The vast majority of the companies don't tell employees the extent of their surveillance.
- 76 percent of the IT professionals said that the companies fear the reaction from their employees if they were to know.
- 11 percent admitted they knew employees would be "horrified" if they knew about the surveillance. (para. 11–22)

In a current and extreme example of employee monitoring, one technology company received consent from a majority of its employees to implant a microchip monitoring device in their bodies. According to a 2017 *New York Times* article (Astor, 2017), employees at Three Square Market, a technology company in Wisconsin, can have a grain-sized chip injected between their thumb and index finger. The chip then enables automatic swiping into the office building and paying for food in the cafeteria with a mere wave of the hand. Most of the employees opted to get the chip implant. In another recent example, Amazon has won patents for an employee tracking device that employees would wear (Reed, 2018, para. 3). The wristband vibrates when the employee makes an error.

In July 2018, Walmart was awarded a patent for a listening system called "Listening to the Frontend" (McGregor, 2018, para. 3). The system captures beeps produced by a scanner and rustling of bags at checkout, and, most alarmingly, the patent mentions that the system could be used to listen to guests' conversations to determine the length of checkout lines.

Walmart indicated the concept was designed as a possible efficiency hack that could help decrease store costs and boost guest satisfaction, writing that "one way to track performance metrics for employees is the use of a system including sound sensors near point of sale ('POS') terminals." The system could "correlate the audio data with an employee that is stationed at the terminal and determine a performance metric for the employee." (McGregor, 2018, para. 10)

In addition to electronic surveillance of various kinds, organizations sometimes ask coworkers to spy on each other. Employees may be asked to report misconduct, ranging from petty theft and unapproved downtime (e.g., overly lengthy breaks or late returns from lunch) to personal tasks being accomplished on company time. According to an article in *The Verge* (Lecher, 2017), in a 2016 lawsuit against Google, an employee claimed that employees were asked to spy on one another to prevent disclosures about the company and its products. An internal email was released during the lawsuit, which suggests a culture of seek and destroy for leakers.

> The internal email was sent . . . with the subject line "the recent leaks." Written by Brian Katz, a former State Department special agent who now runs "investigations" at Google, it begins with a stern warning: "INTERNAL ONLY. REALLY." Katz introduces himself as the head of the "stop leak" team, a group of employees that the lawsuit claims is tasked with tracing the source of information that makes its way to the public. (Lecher, 2017, para. 4)

According to the article, the lawsuit alleges that Google's stop leak team encourages employees to report suspicious activity from their colleagues to a dedicated web address. "Katz allegedly told employees in a webcast 'to look to their left and look to their right,' saying one of those people may be leaking information" (para. 6).

In another current example, Papa Johns was accused of recruiting employees to spy on one another amidst a major public relations crisis. According to an article in *Forbes* (Kirsch, 2018), in the fallout of multiple major public relations crises (the poor handling of the NFL protests, racial slurs uttered by the CEO John Schnatter, and accusations of a toxic culture being created at Papa Johns),

> [John Schnatter] allegedly recruited Papa John's employees to spy on their colleagues. He read workers' emails, according to two sources with knowledge of the episodes, and sometimes conducted business from disposable phones. Schnatter denies that he accessed emails or recruited employees to spy on each other, but admits he occasionally used disposable phones for reasons of "corporate security." (para. 16)

According to a *CSO* article (Fruhlinger, 2018), a Hewlett-Packard spying case is one of the highest-profile examples of such cynical practices. In an effort to uncover a pattern of leaks, the company hired multiple private investigating agencies to spy on its own board members. The case involved gathering the targets' phone records via "pretexting"—essentially, contacting phone companies and convincing them that you are the owner of the phone about which you are asking to gain information. This is a criminal act in California, and the activity eventually ended the careers of several Hewlett-Packard execs.

Most organizations want to monitor their employees' productivity, rule following, and customer/client interactions. In a sense, all supervisors surveil their employees as they do their work. They walk the production line, observe their salespeople interact with customers, and sit in on meetings with clients, among many other supervisory activities. The dark side of surveillance involves a more covert method—a lack of preannouncement of the observation and the creation of an environment where employees are continually reminded that they are not trusted to act according to the organization's best interests when unobserved.

There are myriad problems created in organizations that adopt these heavy-handed practices of surveillance. In addition to the creation of a mistrusting environment, organizations employing these sorts of monitoring strategies, especially when enlisting employees to surveil one another, may create an escalating tit-for-tat pattern of employees reporting on one another or using these policies as a means of harassment or bullying. Further, clients/customers and other key stakeholders may come to view the organization as a hostile and invasive environment. It is also likely that organizations that develop a reputation for covert eavesdropping may actually discourage employees and others from reporting concerns. If the organization is viewed as paranoid or overly controlling, it is unlikely to be perceived as welcoming of critique and expression of dissent or concerns. The covert "listening in" may create a chilling factor on those who might otherwise share information, ideas, or constructive critique.

COMPETITIVE INTELLIGENCE AND ESPIONAGE

Competitive intelligence (CI) is a fact of modern organizational life (with examples dating back at least to the 1800s) with a CI profession emerging in the 1960s. Understanding an organization's competitive environment is often a key component to success. What products, methods of production, and product delivery are being adopted by competitors? What is the next best innovation of competitors? What are they struggling with and what are they thriving in? These sorts of questions can provide information that helps organizations make strategic decisions to remain competitive in their marketplaces.

The line between gathering CI and corporate espionage is somewhat thin, although there are serious legal repercussions for crossing it (see Economic Espionage Act of 1996). Activities falling into these general categories include

- sending secret shoppers into a rival's store to see how it does business,
- hiring a private investigator to lurk around a trade show to see what he or she can overhear,
- interviewing or eavesdropping on a competitor's former or disgruntled current employees,
- calling competitors' suppliers or distributors under the pretense of doing an industry survey to gather intelligence,
- infiltrating a competitor with fake employees,
- hiring away employees from a competitor to obtain specific inside information,
- paying a consultant who has worked for a competitor to disclose secrets,
- using electronic surveillance to eavesdrop on competitors, and
- going through a competitor's trash to discover trade secrets.

A 2012 *New York Times* op-ed by Eamon Javers details the story of the 1990 chocolate wars between candy companies Nestlé and Mars. Javers describes the conflict as follows:

> [The two companies] engaged in an epic corporate war that included a confidential source nicknamed "Deep Chocolate." Former government agents, working through a subcontractor for Nestlé, snatched garbage bags from the Mars headquarters, replacing them with dummy trash bags so the custodial staff wouldn't catch on. Picking through coffee grounds and stale food, they found shredded documents that they were able to painstakingly reconstruct into readable corporate records. (para. 7)

A more current example (Bhuiyan, 2017) concerns accusations that Uber hacked into competitors' databases to collect and store information on employees, financials, business plans, and more and set up surveillance operations in private facilities at hotels and conference venues used by competitors' executive teams for meetings.

Fruhlinger (2018) argues that companies that sell services in CI say that they are legal and aboveboard. They offer services in gathering and analyzing information that is largely public that will affect their clients' fortunes, major organizational plans, and reputation. Common tactics would include researching the background of a rival executive to try to understand his or her motivations and predict his or her behavior. George Chidi (2018), in his description of his career as a corporate spy, suggests that CI begins with an online search strategy to collect, through secondary sources, "everything you can find in the public record about your targets in online business reports, court records, old advertisements, job postings, keyword analytics, blog entries, and elsewhere" (para. 15). The next phase involves "primary intelligence, which means listening to actual people" (para. 15). Chidi says this phase involves "finding the person with the right job title or the right social connection to talk to, and finding enough information about the key intelligence topic to have a clever conversation" (para. 15). He also reports about his use of listening online through surveying with crowdsourcing tools, including Glassdoor, Yelp, RipoffReport.com, and PissedConsumer.com. He finds each of these tools to be somewhat unreliable: Glassdoor overrepresents disgruntled employees; Yelp tends to report overt flattery and insulting commentary, both of which appear unreliable and unreal; and sites such as RipoffReport.com and PissedConsumer.com lean in very obviously biased directions. Chidi argues that he gets more value out of directly contacting people who have posted negative reviews. He also has used reviewing of resumes of a company's applicants as a means to listen to competitors. He says, "The hiring process can be an opportunity to conduct some competitive research. This is an ugly and callous sentiment, but it's up to the job candidate to protect most kinds of competitive information" (para. 39).

"You're a good listener."

Source: Charles Barsotti, www.cartoonstock.com

Because CI is often gathered through direct contact with employees or other insiders, organizations may ramp up their internal surveillance and attune their radar of suspicion in dysfunctional ways. Threatening insiders with punishment if they share any inside information to outsiders and taking steps to prevent eavesdropping by spies are just two of the methods used by organizations to protect themselves from attempts to collect CI. One website,

Bizfluent (Sisk, 2018), offers this advice to organizations to decrease their vulnerabilities, "Emphasize how important it is to refrain from discussing corporate secrets in public or in places where others can overhear, such as outdoor smoking areas. Adding water features, like large outdoor fountains, near these places can make it harder for crafty competitors to eavesdrop" (para. 18).

The Strategic and Competitive Intelligence Professionals (SCIP) organization, established over 30 years ago, is a 501(c)3 nonprofit with a global membership. Its mission (https://www.scip.org/page/AboutSCIP) includes the following:

> Specifically, SCIP provides education and networking opportunities for business professionals working in the rapidly growing field of competitive intelligence (the legal and ethical collection and analysis of information regarding the capabilities, vulnerabilities, and intentions of business competitors). Many SCIP members have backgrounds in marketing, strategy, market research, strategic analysis, science and technology, data science, economics.

The SCIP code of ethics (https://www.scip.org/page/CodeofEthics) requires its members (on penalty of expulsion) to abide by the following rules:

- To comply with all applicable laws, domestic and international
- To accurately disclose all relevant information, including one's identity and organization, prior to all interviews
- To avoid conflicts of interest in fulfilling one's duties
- To provide honest and realistic recommendations and conclusions in the execution of one's duties
- To promote this code of ethics within one's company, with third-party contractors and within the entire profession

One challenge with codes of professional ethics in CI is that many of the individuals involved in some aspect of intelligence gathering may be untrained in CI and unaware of ethical standards and legal requirements of the activity. For example, sending a shift supervisor to a competing restaurant to pose as a customer and gain information about how it performs, what is on the menu, and how it manages customer flow is a form of CI gathering. Grosser, Lopez-Kidwell, Labianca, and Ellwardt (2012) use the example of Anthony Bourdain's report of the use of intelligence working as a head chef:

In *Kitchen Confidential*, Bourdain's memoir of his time working in kitchens throughout New York City, he says:

> "[Bourdain's mentor, 'Bigfoot'] taught me the value of a good, solid and independently reporting intelligence network, providing regular and confirmable

reports that can be verified and cross-checked with other sources. I need to know, you see. Not just what's happening in *my* kitchen, but across the street as well. Is my saucier unhappy? Is the chef across the street ready to make a pass, maybe take him away from me at an inopportune moment? *I need to know!* Is the saucier across the street unhappy? Maybe *he's* available. I need to know that, too. Is the cute waitress who works Saturday nights [having an affair with] my broiler man? Maybe they've got a scam running: food going out without [properly accounting for it]! I have to know everything, you see. What might happen, what could happen, what will happen. And I have to be prepared for it, whatever it is. (p. 101, original emphasis)." (Grosser et al., 2012, p. 54)

An article in the *Journal of Business Ethics* (Rittenburg, Valentine, & Faircloth, 2007) argues that educational programs should "accentuate the gravity of intelligence confidentiality and highlight the ethical dilemmas that personnel might encounter in their jobs." Employees who are involved in CI gathering should be held accountable for the ethical standards of the organization, and those standards should be made quite clear. According to an article in *Webology* (Giustozzi & Van der Veer Martens, 2011), one important domain for CI that is particularly open to inappropriate or unethical behavior is the internet. Here are some examples of murky ethical terrain:

- Misrepresentation can be as simple as someone giving the wrong name in a conversation or as complex as submitting a bid as a nonexistent vendor to a competitor to investigate the competitor's internal environment.
- Blogs, forums, and other social media are open information sources that can be mined to study the public's perception of a company or its competitors. However, fake personas used on these sites to magnify positive reviews contaminate these resources and any analyses based on them.
- CI professionals may turn to CI practitioners, who may also be tempted to use identity-masking software to pose as competitors' customers, business partners, and job applicants.

Aside from the potential for legal liability, corporate espionage and efforts to gather intelligence on competitors may risk the health of strategic organizational listening. The more covert and manipulative the methods of CI gathering, the more risk there is to organizational ethics, reputation, and culture. Listening is more likely to be effective when stakeholders are willing to openly communicate views, perspectives, opinions, information, and experiences. Openness tends to be proportional to trust. When stakeholders trust organizations and the activities within those organizations, they are more likely to be open. Activities that promote a culture of covert intelligence gathering or exploitation of disgruntled stakeholders of competitors are unlikely to promote trust within the organization using such information. Further, the more organizations in any industry or geographic space spy on one another, the easier it is for any given organization to rationalize use of similar tactics, thus, giving rise to an increasing toxicity in the competitive environment, decreasing the likelihood of any future collaborative relationships, and nearly guaranteeing that all organizations will need to take more costly defensive measures.

CONFIRMATION BIAS BY DESIGN

Confirmation bias is a tendency to seek, cherry-pick, and interpret information that confirms our existing beliefs or ideas. Consciously or unconsciously, we can design organizational listening in ways that build in a confirmation bias. Consider the following hypothetical experience at an all-staff meeting in an organization striving for shared governance:

> The leader brings news of a major new initiative. The initiative has been in the works for several months. It is the brainchild of the leader, and she has led the design committee in a series of discussions about it. The committee input was taken in and negotiated, and a final draft of a proposal was produced. In the all-staff meeting, the leader tells those present that "no proposal is perfect" and that "many compromises had to be made." She then shares a long list of approval steps that will be needed for the initiative to get final approval in the organization. Today, she asks for the staff's input on the initiative, again reminding everyone that the committee has been working very hard for several months and this is a good but not perfect proposal. She expresses hope that the group will support the initiative. Questions?

At this stage, the attendee who has reservations about the initiative has three choices: (a) staying silent; (b) voicing praise, objections, and/or concerns; or (c) asking questions. Those who choose silence may do so because it appears that the leader has telegraphed that she is not interested in hearing anything critical or questioning. Such an individual might reasonably wonder what is to be gained by a public questioning or critique. In turn, silence may indicate to the leader that the group is pleased or at least accepting of the proposal, thus, confirming her positive bias. Those who praise the initiative may do so as a way to curry favor with the leader, who is clearly looking for support and endorsement of the initiative. The more praise (faux or real) the leader hears, the more her favorable bias to the proposal as written is confirmed. Some may choose to question or offer concerns. Leaders with strong needs to garner approval for their ideas will often dismiss negatives as part

94

Chapter Five

of a series of inevitable compromises or as a problem to solve later down the road. There is also a chance that the leader is mentally taking names of those who are roadblocks to approval. There could be a price to pay for standing in the way of the leader's pet project. After a few carefully posed concerns are batted away by the leader, silence and acquiescence may return to the meeting. That some concerns were raised but quickly addressed without continued complaint may further reassure the leader that she has not only produced a strong proposal but she's also adequately addressed any concerns that exist.

This example helps illustrate that, despite a leader's best motives to seek input of wider sets of stakeholders, he or she can inadvertently engineer a whole session in a way that discourages genuine critical input from being voiced. One simple sign that this has occurred is when a leader's summary of such sessions includes only the supportive commentary and ignores or minimizes any concerns or questions that were raised. Confirmation bias is part of the dark side of organizational listening because leaders set up barriers to candor and provide megaphones to messages that support favored positions. Further, the very act of holding input-collecting sessions may add to the confirmation that a good process has been followed and helps the leader rationalize her original bias.

MALICIOUS GOSSIP AND INCIVILITY

There are a variety of toxic types of communication within organizations, including malicious gossip and incivility. These forms of workplace hostility have in common that they force witnesses and victims to listen to disturbing, unwelcome, unfriendly, and aggressively presented messages throughout their workday.

All organizations have rumors, and most experience some degree of gossip. Rumor is unverified information that is transmitted throughout a network of individuals trading what they think, know, believe, or wonder about as they make sense of events, activities, information, and people. Gossip is typically of a more personal nature and involves exchange of opinions, commentary, observations or speculation about attributes, experiences, activities, behaviors, orientations, or missteps of individuals who are not party to the conversation. Malicious gossip has a negative orientation, which may target specific individuals with an *intention* to harm reputations and relationships, gain competitive advantage, or drive the victim from the organization. Not only does this behavior harm the targets; it can also intimidate the recipients who are drawn in to listening to the gossip. Negative gossip often will have an implied threat to the recipients that they too may become the target of malicious gossip if they do not comply with the expected behavior of gossiping within the social network (Shallcross, Ramsay, & Barker, 2011).

Incivility in organizations includes rudeness, sarcastic comments, bickering, inappropriate joking, public rebukes, demeaning language, taunting, yelling, and insulting remarks. Such behaviors rarely rise to legal complaints but, nonetheless, have a negative impact on individuals and organizations. A recent article in *Forbes* (Murrell, 2018) presents some of the key negative consequences of organizations rife with incivility:

> Workplace incivility creates a wide range of negative effects including lower employee engagement, reduced work effort, increased worry or anxiety, withdrawal, lower individual satisfaction, and reduced organizational commitment. In extreme cases, affected employees leave the organization and customers who witness incivility take their business elsewhere. Each of these outcomes has negative repercussions on employees, customers and other valuable organizational stakeholders. The long-term impact of workplace incivility can create a toxic culture that is challenging to correct. It can also be financially costly in terms of time spent managing conflict at work and in accounting for increased employee turnover, expensive litigation and the negative impact on the customers' experience and the overall company reputation. (para. 6)

According to an article in the *Chicago Tribune* (Huppke, 2016), a recent study on workplace incivility attributes a rise in such behavior to use of more indirect communication. The study's author, Russell Johnson, argues,

> [a] lot of our communication is done over phone or email. It's hard to understand the intent of an email without any additional language or social or facial cues to go along with it. That creates more ambiguity. And it makes it easier to be uncivil when you're not face-to-face with someone. (para. 9)

Johnson's research focuses on how mental fatigue—often brought on by a person's processing the incivility of others—can increase incivility by turning victims into perpetrators. Because we as witnesses to or recipients of incivility are prompted to spend time and energy decoding a comment that was made and assessing what that comment meant, why the person said it, and how we should respond, a lot of energy is burned, which wears us down over the course of a day. And the more worn down we are mentally, the more likely we are to lose our sense of civility.

These toxic forms of communication in organizations can be emotionally exhausting for targets and listeners. Even for those who are not the targets of gossip and incivility, the ambient hostility and tit-for-tat escalation of aggression in the workplace manifest a dark side of listening. Some individuals serve in the role of toxin handlers in organizations. These are the people most actively engaged in dealing with negative and toxic emotions. Peter Frost (2004) discusses the important role of "toxin handlers" in providing empathetic capacity to notice when and how painful situations turn toxic. Frost argues that toxin handlers "step into situations at work to dissipate or to buffer the toxins so that those who are in harm's way are rescued or protected and can get on with doing their organizational work" (p. 115). These individuals bear a good deal of the load of listening to victims of gossip, witnesses to incivility, and those stressed by rumors. Although they certainly do the work of providing emotional support in organizations and, thereby, play a positive role, they also are at high risk for burnout and exit if the wider pattern of negative talk and incivility continues unabated.

FOSTERING DISBELIEF AND DISTRUST OF WHAT IS HEARD

Some organizational cultures foster a distrustful environment through routinely casting doubt on the reliability of individuals' perspectives and frequently portraying challengers as insincere or untrustworthy. When organizational leaders argue that employees are irrational or deceitful, customers/clients are merely complainers, experts are political hacks, or protesters are hired hands, they rationalize a dismissive orientation to negative input.

A major dysfunction in some approaches to listening to negative feedback in organizations concerns the questioning of motives. When providers of input have impure motives, leaders may find cover to ignore the substance of what is provided. A recent viral video of a Walmart employee publicly quitting his job serves as a poignant example. The seventeen-year-old employee quit his job by making the following announcement over the store intercom: "'Attention all shoppers, associates and management, I would like to say to all of you today that nobody should work here, ever. . . . Our managers will make promises and never keep them'" (Hess, 2018, para. 4). During his remarks, the employee noted that he had been working for Walmart for over a year and a half, and he calls out his assistant manager for insulting him.

It would be very easy for the managers at this store to disregard the claims made by the quitting employee as a mere rant that deserved no further follow-up. They could easily question his motives for the public disclosures as retaliatory. Indeed, it is possible that this incident was nothing more than a disgruntled employee's desire to get even with his boss. However, it is also possible that, despite the poor choice of his means to vent his concerns, he may have something of value to offer this organization. He may have voiced the truth about harsh or inappropriate treatment. He may have been brought to the point of such a public and angry action due to pent-up frustration from being ignored for some time before his outburst. However, it is much easier for managers in such circumstances to excuse themselves from any examination of his complaints because they can dismiss them as irrational and unprofessional. Their listening is portrayed as victimhood; they were forced to endure the outburst.

In the political realm, the term "astroturfing" has become synonymous with fake protest and faux outrage that is not borne of genuine political citizen expression. This term is used to describe protest that is not a grassroots, spontaneous expression by citizens but, rather, is a sponsored political action by some advocacy group or organization. The goal of astroturfing is to create a sense of widespread public support for some political position when it may not exist in reality. This tactic is used by numerous organizations and companies with various motivations to advocate for policies or laws or as a public relations strategy.

The labeling of citizen protests as "astroturf activism" promotes a doubting of the content of criticisms as well as the motivations of those who choose to demonstrate. During the controversial Supreme Court confirmation hearings for Brett Kavanaugh, President Trump accused demonstrators of being paid and fake. He tweeted, "The very rude elevator screamers are paid professionals only looking to make Senators look bad. Don't fall for it! Also, look at all of the professionally made identical signs. Paid for by Soros and others. These are not signs made in the basement from love! #Troublemakers" (Trump, 2018). Such accusations encourage the dismissal of protests as disingenuous.

Whenever organizations intermingle assessment of critics' motivations with evaluation of the content of what they share, the likely result is to foster distrust of the information that is heard. If you add to this the politicization of information, the effect can be devastating to strategic listening. In an article about scientific communication in a "post-truth society" (Iyengar & Massey, 2019), the authors make the claim that

> whenever scientific findings clash with a person or group's political agenda, be it conservative (as with climate science and immigration) or liberal (as with genetically modified foods and vaccination risks), scientists can expect to encounter a targeted campaign of fake news, misinformation, and disinformation in response, no matter how clearly the information is presented or how carefully and convincingly it is framed. (p. 5)

These authors argue that political polarization results in the rejection of information and arguments that clash with an adopted worldview. Rather than process information dispassionately, individuals may resort to a pattern of reasoning focused on protection of their closely held beliefs and values from any threat. "The upshot is that when evidence clashes with individuals' partisan loyalties, it is either dismissed or distorted, thereby impeding the diffusion of scientific findings" (p. 3). Similar suspicion may fall on sources of information even when politics is not relevant. Factions of stakeholders in organizations may be associated with biases (e.g., strengthening of unions/ defeat of unions, pro small business/pro industry giants, and client focused/ efficiency focused) and polarized views that pervade an industry, location, or resources. Association of data, research, information, or documentation with some perceived biased source can often result in a lack of serious listening.

In some cases, bad actors in organizations may purposefully discredit individuals as untrustworthy or biased to discourage others from listening to them. Whistle-blowers very frequently get this sort of treatment. A 2017 *Forbes* article (Higginbottom, 2017) cites a report that reveals that whistle-blowers are often demonized and sometimes portrayed as mentally ill. *Retraction Watch*'s (Oransky, 2018) interview with a whistle-blowing expert, Kathy Ahern, reveals how whistle-blowers are systematically gaslighted in ways that erode their own sense of psychological security and trust in the organization. In the beginning, they believe that they are being listened to, but later they are betrayed by the very people to whom they have reported some wrongdoing:

> The common narrative of whistleblowers is that at first they believe the repeated reassurances of kindly institutional officers. However, over months or years, the whistleblowers find that inevitably their expectations of due process are betrayed by an inexplicable incompetence at every turn. The whistleblower becomes anxious, despairing and mistrustful—symptoms that mirror paranoia. However, these symptoms are not the result of delusions, but are a normal response to repeated promises and betrayals. (para. 10)

Whistle-blowers are often bullied, and their motivations and abilities to make judgments are frequently questioned. They become more paranoid after coworkers express disbelief and doubt about their claims. According to Ahern, "Wherever the whistleblower turns, they are met with the two-step of reassurance that their concerns are taken seriously and inexplicable incompetence in investigating allegations of reprisals" (para. 18). She identifies other common red flags of this process:

- Reprimands and complaints only start after the alleged misconduct was reported.
- Proactive steps to prevent reprisals are not undertaken.
- The institution downgrades allegations of reprisals to a grievance procedure, which does not enable wrongs to be redressed.

- The response is inadequate and includes willful blindness to evidence and stonewalling.
- The whistleblower's experiences are denied, such as unfair treatment being called a "personality clash" or "miscommunication."
- Supervisors, HR, union reps and/or senior executives fail to intervene in retaliatory actions. (para. 19)

In such cases, faux listening is used as a means to both camouflage the organizations' disinterest in addressing the core report of wrongdoing and discredit the whistle-blower. Organizational officials gather information from whistle-blowers about their concerns or complaints and then use it against them to portray them as irrational, paranoid, or isolated and ill informed.

ROUTINIZED INATTENTIVE LISTENING

Most of the dysfunctional listening discussed in this chapter so far concerns the use of listening for some ill intent or being related to a suspect motivation. A far more common dark listening practice concerns listening that is overly scripted, routinized, and inattentive. Those who occupy organizational roles assigned to listen to customers/clients, employees, or community members who typically present problems, complaints, concerns, and flaws in service, products, or programs fall into patterns of inactive listening. Lower-level employees are often assigned to receive common complaints and concerns that are viewed by the organization as currently unresolvable or unreasonable. Employees who daily hear such complaints quickly become numb to hearing the variety of expressions of the same themes. They often are trained on how to display signals of sincere listening, allocate a rote response, and perhaps provide a palliative measure or gesture (e.g., coupon or free product sample). Although this sort of listening is not "dark" due to mal-intention, it does real harm to the organization and the stakeholders. Stakeholders lose an opportunity to have a concern genuinely heard. Organizations run the risk of having a variety of similar-sounding complaints put into a common box when there could be important nuanced information and feedback that is missed or disregarded. The combined outcome of these two situations is that core causes of problems are left unaddressed and without remedy, forcing others to endure them in the future.

Not all issues and concerns can be immediately resolved. Clients at understaffed government agencies will experience long waits; customers at stores with recalled food items will be disappointed to see unavailable items; community members seeking certifications, licenses, or documents from highly regulated organizations will need to endure lengthy paperwork or bureaucratic processes. Although these sorts of negative experiences may not be immediately solvable by the people and organizations on the front line, there are ways to be proactive in dealing with them (e.g., posting signs about wait times, advertising alternatives, and providing guidebooks and tip sheets) that could be adapted to clients/customers based on the feedback received about frustrations, concerns, and information needs. Listening carefully to the experiences of these people and learning from them is strategic. One type of dark-side listening occurs when listening involves little more than a nod of the head, a disinterested look, and a routine explanation of the general rule or process.

CONCLUSION

This chapter illustrates the dark side of listening. Listening can be difficult, malicious, disingenuous, and cynical. The ways in which listening is designed and executed can promote a hostile, cynical, and unethical organizational culture and may erode relationships within and between organizations and between organizations and their stakeholders. As with most processes in organizations, any particular approach can be used in service of positive or negative goals. These examples illustrate that the mere act of listening—of hearing and comprehending what someone has said—does not necessarily mean ethical, strategic, and positive outcomes for individuals or organizations.

REFERENCES

Astor, M. (2017, July 25). Microchip implants for employees? One company says yes. *New York Times*. Retrieved from https://www.nytimes.com/2017/07/25/technology/microchips-wisconsin-company-employees.html

Bhuiyan, J. (2017, December 15). Here's the letter alleging Uber spied on individuals for competitive intelligence. *Vox*. Retrieved from https://www.recode.net/2017/12/15/16782534/alphabet-waymo-uber-self-driving-lawsuit-jacobs-letter-surveillance

Chidi, G. (2018). Confessions of a corporate spy. *Inc*. Retrieved from https://www.inc.com/magazine/201302/george-chidi/confessions-of-a-corporate-spy.html

Frost, P. J. (2004). Handling toxic emotions: New challenges for leaders and their organizations. *Organizational Dynamics, 33*(2), 111–127.

Fruhlinger, J. (2018, July 2). What is corporate espionage? Inside the murky world of private spying. *CSO*. Retrieved from https://www.csoonline.com/article/3285726/security/what-is-corporate-espionage-inside-the-murky-world-of-private-spying.html

Giustozzi, E. S., & Van der Veer Martens, B. (2011, December). The new competitive intelligence agents: "Programming" competitive intelligence ethics into corporate cultures. *Webology*, *8*(2), Article 88. Retrieved from http://www.webology.org/2011/v8n2/a88.html

Grosser, T. J., Lopez-Kidwell, V., Labianca, G., & Ellwardt, L. (2012). Hearing it through the grapevine: Positive and negative workplace gossip. *Organizational Dynamics*, *41*(1), 52–61.

Hess, A. (2018, December 14). 17-year-old Walmart employee quits over store intercom: "Nobody should work here, ever." *CNBC*. Retrieved from https://www.cnbc.com/2018/12/14/walmart-employee-quits-over-intercom-nobody-should-work-here-ever.html

Higginbottom, K. (2017, February 18). The price of being a whistleblower. *Forbes.* Retrieved from https://www.forbes.com/sites/karenhigginbottom/2017/02/18/the-price-of-being-a-whistleblower/#5259f1035b52

Huppke, R. (2016, August 12). Incivility at work is on the rise. *Chicago Tribune*. Retrieved from https://www.chicagotribune.com/business/careers/ct-huppke-work-advice-0814-biz-20160812-column.html

Iyengar, S., & Massey, D. S. (2019). Scientific communication in a post-truth society. *Proceedings of the National Academy of Sciences*, *116*(6), 7656–7661. Retrieved from https://www.pnas.org/content/early/2018/11/21/1805868115

Javers, E. (2012, October 24). Spies & co. *New York Times*. Retrieved from https://www.nytimes.com/2012/10/25/opinion/corporate-espionage-american-style.html

Kirsch, N. (2018, July 19). The inside story of Papa John's toxic culture. *Forbes*. Retrieved from https://www.forbes.com/sites/forbesdigitalcovers/2018/07/19/the-inside-story-of-papa-johns-toxic-culture/#6992ae123019

Lecher, C. (2017, May 22). An internal Google email shows how the company cracks down on leaks. *The Verge*. Retrieved from https://www.theverge.com/2017/5/22/15666672/google-lawsuit-email-stop-leaks

Matyszczyk, C. (2018, June 21). In a startling new study, companies admit to spying on employees far more than employees realize. *Inc.* Retrieved from https://www.inc.com/chris-matyszczyk/study-shows-how-much-companies-spy-on-employees.html

McGregor, J. (2018, July 12). What Walmart's patent for audio surveillance could mean for its workers. *Washington Post.* Retrieved from https://www.washingtonpost.com/business/2018/07/12/what-walmarts-patent-audio-surveillance-could-mean-its-workers/?noredirect=on&utm_term=.ce125f1697ee

Murrell, A. (2018, July 16). Stopping the downward spiral of workplace incivility. *Forbes*. Retrieved from https://www.forbes.com/sites/audreymurrell/2018/07/16/stopping-the-downward-spiral-of-workplace-incivility/#1a38933f54ef

Oransky, I. (2018, July 30). How institutions gaslight whistleblowers—and what can be done. *Retraction Watch*. Retrieved from https://retractionwatch.com/2018/07/30/how-institutions-gaslight-whistleblowers-and-what-can-be-done/

Reed, R. (2018, March 2). Workplace monitoring gets personal, and employees fear it's too close for comfort. They're right. *Chicago Tribune*. Retrieved from https://www.chicagotribune.com/business/columnists/reed/ct-biz-amazon-workplace-privacy-dilemma-robert-reed-0304-story.html

Rittenburg, T. L., Valentine, S. R., & Faircloth, J. B. (2007). An ethical decision-making framework for competitive intelligence gathering. *Journal of Business Ethics, 70*(3), 235–245.

Shallcross, L., Ramsay, S., & Barker, M. (2011). The power of malicious gossip. *Australian Journal of Communication, 38*(1), 45–67. Retrieved from https://research-repository.griffith.edu.au/bitstream/handle/10072/53052/85406_1.pdf?sequence=1&isAllowed=y

Sisk, A. (2018, August 16). Corporate espionage definition. *Bizfluent*. Retrieved from https://bizfluent.com/about-6742556-corporate-espionage-definition.html

Trump, D. J. [@realDonaldTrump]. (2018, October 25). The very rude elevator screamers are paid professionals only looking to make Senators look bad. Don't fall for it! Also, look at all of the professionally made identical signs. Paid for by Soros and others. These are not signs made in the basement from love! #Troublemakers [Tweet]. Retrieved from https://twitter.com/realDonaldTrump/status/1048196883464818688

ANOTHER RESOURCE

Fehringer, D., & Hohhof, B. (Eds.). (2006). *Competitive intelligence ethics: Navigating the gray zone.* San Antonio, TX: Strategic and Competitive Intelligence Professionals.

Chapter Six

Appraisal of Strategic Organizational Listening

By this point, if you are now convinced that strategic organizational listening is important, you may now wonder what steps ought to be taken first to systematically review and evaluate your organization's current capacity and quality of listening. This chapter describes the scope and steps in auditing an organization's or unit's values, principles, processes, practices, infrastructure, techniques, and outcomes related to listening. The chapter provides a guide to leaders to systematically review eight key domains of strategic organizational listening. This APPRAISE audit tool provides a comprehensive approach to assessing listening in an organization:

1. **A**ctivities and practices of listening
2. **P**roblems related to listening
3. **P**rinciples that guide listening
4. **R**esources that support listening
5. **A**pproaches to listening
6. **I**nsights gained through listening
7. **S**atisfaction of stakeholders with listening
8. **E**spoused values related to listening

The chapter first overviews the means to appraise listening in the organization and introduces key planning questions that should be addressed before data is collected. Second, the chapter introduces five general methods that may be used to examine and evaluate the current state of strategic listening in your organization. In that section, specific sample tools are presented. Finally, the chapter introduces each of the key areas for a thorough listening appraisal. Any given organization or organizational unit may wish to conduct an overall appraisal of listening including each of the eight areas or focusing on a single area or a subset of areas.

APPRAISAL PROCESS

This chapter provides a framework for a process to appraise your organization's strategic listening. Before I develop the specific framework, I will first introduce key concepts related to doing this sort of appraisal. To appraise any organization's strategic listening, the evaluator will have to practice effective listening. To assess listening, whether engaging in a thorough, detailed, data-based overview of all aspects of strategic listening or merely taking a pulse reading of a subset of activities or diagnosing problems in a particular unit, evaluators must be good listeners. Some organizations involved in this appraisal process that have reason to believe they are not practiced and skilled listeners may wisely recruit external consultants or peer evaluators with strong listening skills.

The process of appraising the strategic listening activity and quality should begin with thoughtful planning. It is important to begin the process by posing and answering a set of key questions:

- Who is going to use the data and for what purposes?
- What types of data are most useful for those people and goals?
- Who are the stakeholders in the evaluation; that is, whose stakes are threatened or in play?
- Who needs to be involved in the appraisal process?
- What time frame and resources are available?

In chapter 1, I argued that listening can and should fall into a category of strategic behavior in organizations and that, rather than merely randomly listening as a generally good practice, organizations should listen with connection to plans, goals, and decisional frameworks. I further argued that the best strategic listening goals for organizations are to ensure that an organization's attention is directed toward vital information and input to enable learning, questioning of key assumptions, interrogating decisions, and self-critical analysis. This sort of strategic thinking should also guide the appraisal of strategic listening. In essence, organizations deciding to undertake an appraisal of current listening will be performing a formative evaluation. A formative evaluation is typically aimed at providing information for program improvement, modification, and management.

As the appraisal team members consider the purpose and goals of this process, it is critical that they develop an understanding of how the information, interpretations, and conclusions will be used in the organization. There are numerous possibilities; here are a few of them:

- To assess a specific listening activity or process
- To describe a full range of listening activities and processes within a unit or the whole organization
- To make those responsible for listening activities more aware of their successes and challenges (where things are going well and where there needs to be improvement)
- To reallocate resources (budget, infrastructure, personnel, and time) to a different set of listening activities in a specific area or for the whole organization
- To identify common listening lapses across the organization or within specific units and with specific stakeholders
- To guide development of a set of new plans, priorities, and infrastructure to support listening
- To identify ways that the organizational culture is supportive or unsupportive of strategic listening and determine better ways to foster a strategic listening culture
- To assess and correct lapses in the organization's listening principles, values, and ethics

Clearly, these goals vary, from extremely ambitious to more developmental. Whatever the goals of assessment are, the team members will be better prepared to make good evaluation design decisions if they know what they are trying to learn and to what ultimate purpose these data and interpretations will be put.

It is also important to determine the primary audience for the results of the appraisal. The consumers of the information, interpretations, and recommendations will likely vary in what they find persuasive and useful. Some stakeholders may respond well to hard, quantifiable data, trends, and statistical analyses. Others will find benchmarked data comparing peer organizations most impressive. Still others will be engaged with narrative examples that vividly illustrate problems, challenges, and successes. When presented with challenging, critical, or disconfirming claims and evidence, some audiences might suffer from some of the very issues I've noted in previous chapters. For example, if what is presented is personally threatening in some way, they may become defensive or doubtful and may discount it. This is one reason that stakeholder buy-in to the process of this evaluation is necessary. If the goals of the evaluation are made clear and as nonthreatening as possible, the likelihood that those with insight to real and perceived problems and lapses will readily identify and act on them. One way to encourage a positive start to this sort of process is to ask every stakeholder or group to identify two or three examples of strong listening. This appreciative inquiry technique can lower defensive postures and provide input about successful examples. Once examples are collected, they can be analyzed in terms of why they were so successful and what elements contributed to positive outcomes. Such analyses can provide clues to what might be replicated elsewhere in the organization or what routines and resources might need to be provided in a more consistent manner.

As plans are made to collect information about listening, the appraisal team should involve stakeholders who have a variety of vantage points on the organization's listening capacities, practices, activities, and outcomes. Further, a diverse set of stakeholders should be invited to serve as sources of information about the organization's listening. More will be learned in the appraisal process through involvement of individuals and groups that have a stake in the organization's listening and may have unique experiences in engaging with the organization. What constitutes "diverse" in any given organization will vary. Consideration should be given to including stakeholders whose characteristics range in the ways shown in Figure 6.1.

Internal -- External

Higher-level Leadership ------------------------------------- Front-line Staff

Staff function -- Line Function

Technical -- Content

Lengthy Affiliations -------------------------------------- New Affiliations

Highly Satisfied --- Very Unsatisfied

Customer-Facing ------------------------------------- Production-focused

Volunteer Labor -- Paid Labor

High Specialization/Training ------------------ Moderate/Low Spec/Training

Figure 6.1.

Availability of resources and time will also be important determinants of the scope and methods of a listening appraisal project. Some methods are more labor intensive, expensive, and time consuming to execute. These factors should be considered when deciding the level of investment being made into appraisal. Methods involving collection and analysis of detailed individual cases and narratives are likely to take more time and personnel and require significant analysis to interpret. Methods that are more comprehensive but may be partially automated or take advantage of existing metrics or routine data collection can provide useful indicators; however, they may lack the depth of information required to meet some goals.

METHODS FOR APPRAISAL

There are countless methods available to appraise the value, quality, and range of listening in an organization. Rather than attempt to compile a complete listing in this chapter, I will focus on five general types of methods. There are many variations on how each method could be deployed in an appraisal of listening.

Observation. Listening may occur in many locations in any organization. They may be physical spaces (e.g., retail or service delivery locations, meetings with publics, and all-staff meetings) or virtual spaces (e.g., customer service call-in lines, online chats, and Q&A submissions). It is likely that supervisors fairly routinely observe employees as they encounter stakeholders in these spaces. They may even include in their supervision focused attention on the listening behaviors of these employees. As part of a purposeful appraisal of listening for the organization, these observations can be made more uniform and structured. Useful observations will be carefully designed to detect and provide information that can help evaluate the manner, timing, quality, and outcomes of listening. Observations can yield insight to decision-makers about the real-time ways in which listening is undertaken and provide specific examples that may be especially clarifying. When evaluators focus on the listening activity itself, as opposed to other practices (e.g., problem solving, instruction giving, and information dissemination), they can learn much about how well listening is done and how it is received and evaluated. To be successful, the evaluators must be sensitized to specific behaviors, dynamics, and orientations of listeners. This means that time must be invested in training evaluators who carry out observations so they know what to watch for and to ensure that everyone is using the same rubric as they do their observations. Appendix A is a sample of an observational guide, which may be adapted and used to make sense of listening activity in your organization. Application of this general example must be customized to the specific type of listening activity, the context for listening, and the type of stakeholders who are engaged in listening.

Archival review. Often, it is useful to review the formal written policies, routines, scripts, instructions, documents, and reports related to listening in the organization. Such documents could include information used in training of employees, policies used by various units to guide the way they engage with stakeholders, ethics guidelines for those involved in gathering competitive intelligence, and reports evaluating points of contact and levels of satisfaction of various stakeholders. This review should include a comprehensive search for formalized language that indicates to employees and other stakeholders the value the organization has for listening activities and the commitments the organization has made to listening. Further, previous reviews of organizational successes or failures of listening should also be included.

Interviews. Talking with people is one of the best ways to learn how they think, what they believe, and what they've experienced. While more time consuming than other methods, the yield of detailed stories of experience is quite valuable. In interviews, we can learn not only what people perceive but also why they have come to those perceptions. We can probe answers, ask for additional detail in stories, and respond to presented issues with additional clarifying questions in real time. Of course, as noted earlier, some of the same dynamics related to listening discussed throughout this book may be likely to occur throughout an interview process. As we invite stakeholders to provide their input; go through the process of asking for perspectives, views, opinions, and experiences; and then listen and record what we hear, we can replicate our own worst practices of listening. Therefore, it is critical that the interviewers be highly skilled at creating rapport, building trust, and listening intentionally to those who are interviewed.

In a major appraisal process, a team of interviewers should be involved in creating an effective interview guide that has a standard set of questions. The interviewers should practice using the interview guide and have ready tactics to provoke specific examples, elaborated explanations, and details. The goal of interviews is to get beyond metrics, ratings, and generalities and get into details, stories, and individual experiences and reactions. The richer the stories and examples, the more useful the interview data will be. Of course, it is possible to solicit detailed stories with a questionnaire, but the interviewer would not be able to probe the stories and ask for elaboration or further explanation of details. An example of an interview guide can be found in appendix B, which may be adapted and used to make sense of listening activity in your organization.

In addition to one-on-one interviews, it may be useful to conduct focus group interviews with groups of stakeholders. Focus groups can certainly create efficiencies by allowing the evaluators to talk to more people more quickly than it would take to complete individual interviews. However, the more significant gain in using focus groups is that, if done well, groups of stakeholders will often trigger ideas, thoughts, and examples in each other. They also may be prompted to disclose more if they feel that their experiences are shared by others in the group. Creating rules of disclosure that promote candor, supportiveness, and confidentiality will be important for some sets of stakeholders. In focus groups, the facilitator does not conduct an interview; rather, he or she starts a discussion about a topic. If the facilitator is able to introduce a topic in a way that creates a lively discussion among the participants, much can be learned by hearing the back-and-forth of comments and storytelling.

Questionnaires. Questionnaires are a common tool used to learn individuals' perceptions, evaluations, priorities, and preferences. Questionnaires can be constructed in ways that provide easily comparable responses; develop evidence of most and least common opinions; and enable sophisticated analyses for describing how sets of experiences, opinions, and preferences relate to one another. There are many advantages to quantitative ratings, scores, and opinion data, including that they are relatively easy to store, analyze, and manipulate. There are also drawbacks. Quantitative survey data provides a summary of respondents' complex ideas and perceptions. When using questionnaires to evaluate listening, evaluators are forcing respondents to generalize from a wide range of individual reactions, experiences, and preferences, which compels respondents to leave nuance and context to the side. As we read summary evaluations like those in questionnaires, it is important to be mindful of the effects of summarization. For example, whenever we ask respondents to give an "average rating" of their experience with an organization or a specific type of experience (e.g., listening), evaluators are asking them to think across several individual interactions and imagine what is typical. However, most respondents will recall the more unique (and perhaps extreme) interactions more vividly and may be very poor at estimating what a typical experience is. One way to avoid the summarization problem is to ask respondents to focus on a specific encounter or experience (perhaps the most recent case). Although the most recent encounter may have been atypical for that respondent, the collection of "most recent encounters" across the sample will give a better overall representation of what stakeholders experience in general. Appendix C is a bank of questionnaire items, which could be used to explore the various elements of the APPRAISE audit as described in later sections of this chapter.

Reflection and stock taking. Evaluators will certainly need to thoroughly review all data collected through archival, observations, interviews, and questionnaire methods. However, before that data is collected, it may be useful for organizational leaders, decision-makers, and supervisors to devote time to simply discussing what they think is and is not working well in terms of the organization's practices, systems, approaches, and culture as they relate to listening. Rather than focus on a systematic evaluation, stock taking is more of a conversation about what those who are involved in a process intuitively think about it. This conversation could include a candid self-description of how listening works in an organization and what is done well or what could be improved or added.

ANALYSIS AND INTERPRETATION

Assigning meaning to data can be difficult and complex. Data does not "speak for itself" but, rather, requires interpretation and appropriate application. "The Parable of the Frog and the Scientist" (Patton, 1982) offers some good lessons:

> Once there was a scientist who was studying how far frogs could jump. He yelled at a frog, "jump!" and the frog jumped 10 feet.
>   Then he cut off one leg of the frog. He yelled "jump!" and the frog jumped five feet.
>   Then he cut off a second leg. He yelled "jump!" and the frog jumped one foot.
>   Then, he cut off a third leg. He yelled "jump!" and the frog jumped four inches.
>   Then, he cut off a fourth leg. He yelled "jump!" and the frog did not move.
>   The scientist concluded: When you cut off four legs of a frog, the frog becomes deaf! (p. 175)

As you can see from this humorous tale, it is easy to fit facts to a conclusion and to draw wildly implausible conclusions from raw data. It is important to systematically review all data collected and to test all interpretations and conclusions carefully against alternatives and framed within the questions that are the focus of the appraisal. Once data is collected, it is important to pause and recall the purposes and guiding questions of the appraisal. Once the team members are reminded of the purposes for the appraisal, they should separate the data into each of the following levels:

- Findings—the facts of the case; raw data
- Interpretations—explanations offered about the findings; speculations about the interrelationships, causes, and reasons for findings
- Judgments—values brought to bear about good and bad or positive and negative
- Recommendations—suggested course of action

Interpreting data will be aided by using the key questions and purposes of the appraisal to frame the data. For example, if evaluators find many cases of limited accessibility, repeated dismissal of complaints, or inconsistent follow-through of identified problems, they should try to frame these examples in terms of key guiding interests of the appraisal. In this case, it might be to identify common listening lapses across the organization, within specific units, or with specific stakeholders.

Once the appraisal team members determine how their findings shed light on specific questions that were being explored, it will be important to determine whether the evidence supports positive or negative judgments. To make judgments, the appraisal team must apply values and principles to the observations that are collected. These values should be known before the evaluation process is started. Appraisers should have a sense of the tolerance level for lapses of listening, the goals for satisfaction of stakeholders, and the principles embraced in the organization for hearing candid and even critical feedback. For example, if leaders operate on a principle that critique should always be accompanied by useful and productive recommendations, they will evaluate negative commentary as less useful if the critics do not propose solutions to identified problems. On the other hand, if the organization's listening principles support being open to all critique—no matter from whom, with what intention, or whether it is paired with remedy—evaluations of lapses in listening to negative feedback will likely be judged as a problem to be solved.

Development of recommendations is the final step in appraisal. As with earlier steps, this step should be framed within the original questions and purposes of the evaluation. One straightforward way to create recommendations is to take each key topic or question in turn, list a set of data-based conclusions and interpretations, and present a set of recommendations. Findings, interpretations, and recommendations need to be sensitive to what "can be done" and the local culture and view of the activities being evaluated. Appraisers may wish to present a range of possible recommendations. Recommendations that challenge the organization may be presented in terms of a range of options, from the more incremental to the more profound. A thorough appraisal process will present at least a general assessment of the level of demand on resources that each recommendation would entail.

AREAS FOR LISTENING APPRAISAL

The APPRAISE audit involves review of listening in each of the key domains listed at the beginning of this chapter. This section reviews the content that should be assessed within each area.

Activities and practices of listening. Essentially, any task, process, or interaction involving an opportunity to listen to stakeholders holds potential information for the appraisal team. There are a number of key activities and practices mentioned in previous chapters that should be the focus of review. As discussed in chapter 1, listening is an example of an information-gathering process. Examination of the 10 steps from chapter 1 involved in information processing may provide critical information about how well the organization or unit is able to assess its needs for information and to collect and distribute it:

1. How does the unit recognize the need for information?
2. How does the unit recognize the need for accurate and complete information?
3. To what extent does the unit formulate questions based on needs?
4. How does the unit identify potential sources of information?
5. How does the unit develop search strategies?
6. Which sources, including computer-based and other technology, are used?
7. How is information evaluated?
8. What methods are used to organize information for application?
9. How is information integrated into existing bodies of knowledge?
10. To what degree is the information used in critical thinking and problem solving in the organization?

Using the methods outlined in this chapter, a check of strengths and weaknesses of processes across these steps can yield important insights. The appraisal team will want to assess how each of these steps is undertaken in critical areas for listening across the organization. Each unit involved in the appraisal should begin with stock taking and archival review of its own process—using these ten steps as the general template—and then design interview and questionnaire methods to further assess how important stakeholders perceive and experience the components of the process.

Although the above evaluation will reveal strengths and weaknesses in routine information gathering, other important nonroutine listening activities also should be reviewed. Chapter 1 discussed the importance of handling both highly structured and unstructured data and input in listening. It will be important for units and organizations to determine whether they are able to handle unusual forms of input—stories, protests and demonstrations, and social media campaigns—that are unexpected, disorganized, and evolving in real time. Oftentimes, such episodes of heightened unstructured input will come at a time of crisis or other difficult circumstance for the stakeholder or the organization. Examination of cases of difficult conversations through archival methods, interviews, or stock taking of processes may be used to train individuals in the organization to handle such situations. Units should develop a set of methods to review their routines and sample cases for listening activities designed for

- collecting critique, concerns, and dissent;
- collecting bad news;
- collecting early warnings of potentially negative consequences; and
- collecting views, perspectives, opinions, and information about what people need.

The appraisal team members should aim to discover how these sorts of listening activities happen. Key questions raised in chapter 2 should be answered, including the following:

- What is the setting, context, and timing of these activities?
- Who gets asked? By whom? Where? In front of whom?
- Who gets routinely ignored?
- What are these individuals asked to provide?
- What happens in these sessions?
- Are there routines of listening that have become meaningless and void of sincerity?
- Are there unmonitored channels (e.g., "tell us what you think" or suggestion boxes)?
- Is technology used in appropriate and useful ways to surface important insights?

Problems related to listening. A key goal for any appraisal process is identifying problems and weaknesses. In the introduction to this book, several cases of listening failures were presented. An important stock-taking question for any organization is, "When has listening failed in this organization?" As the appraisal team members set out to identify, analyze, and make conclusions about listening failures, they should adopt a focus on learning lessons, rather than placing blame or identifying poor listeners. To identify where processes have broken down and appropriate actions were not taken, it will be important for participants and witnesses to provide candid descriptions of what occurred. Appraisers will need to gain insight into the mind-set of individuals who may have dismissed information, failed to follow up on warnings, or even purposefully or inadvertently discouraged reporting of problems or bad news. Key questions for appraisers to review follow:

- What examples can be found of extremely poor listening in the unit?
- What are the major events or activities along a timeline of these cases?
- Who knew of information that was not treated in an appropriate way?

- Why were important information, perspectives, and experiences not channeled in appropriate ways?
- What biases, assumptions, or ineffective screening were in operation in these cases?
- What structural barriers (e.g., too many layers, too many "middle steps," and unavailable channels to surface concerns) inhibited or prevented important and relevant information from getting to the right person or unit?
- What motivations or concerns influenced those whose actions contributed to the listening failure? Were they worried about their job security? About consequences for taking action?

In addition to looking for particular examples or cases where listening has apparently failed, it is also important for the appraisal team to gather evidence of systemic or chronic problems of listening failures or dysfunctional practices related to listening. As earlier chapters have noted, there are numerous contexts wherein listening may be done lightly, ineffectively, without purpose, or with toxic or unethical practices. Using methods described above, appraisers should explore routine activities and systems related to the following:

- Reporting bad news, problems, and concerns upward in the organization
- Problematic or absent routines of leaders and decision-makers in calling for and reviewing objections, concerns, and potential problems
- Chronic failures in addressing the circulation of rumors or gossip, which is damaging to individuals, units, stakeholders, or the organization
- Missed opportunities to gather stakeholders' beliefs, attitudes, understandings, needs, and desires
- Evidence of continual breakdowns in communication across groups and units in the organization

Principles that guide listening. The introduction to this book argues that listening may be approached as a strategy, rather than as a mere courtesy or vapid public relations tactic. Listening is something organizations should learn to accomplish in effective, intentional, ongoing, and practical ways. The opening chapters of this book compared an individual skill of listening to a public relations listening approach to a strategic focus of organizational listening. A strategic focus involves an effective process for interrogating evidence, identifying and understanding implications, and challenging status quo thinking in light of what is heard. The overall approach to listening in a given unit or organization involves basic guiding principles. Principles involve strategic intention, authenticity, and ethics.

As appraisal team members work to describe and assess the listening principles of a particular unit or the whole organization, they may wish to characterize the ways that various groups of stakeholders understand what listening principles are in play. Through asking stakeholders for their inferences about principles that guide listening, appraisers should work to identify the following:

- How are the key principles of listening described by stakeholders (e.g., strategic, proactive, reactive, ethical, or authentic)?
- Do stakeholders believe that their input and feedback are genuinely desired and considered important in the unit or organization?
- Is the focus of gathering ideas, perspectives, input, and feedback to improve the ways in which the unit or organization operates?
- Do stakeholders believe that their input and feedback are used to inform decision-making in the unit or organization?

The appraisal team may also be able to assess, through archival, observation, questionnaire, and interview methods, whether listening in the unit or organization is done with humility, genuine curiosity, and an intention to learn. As discussed in the introduction to this book, appraisers can ask whether listening is directed toward vital information and input to enable learning, questioning of key assumptions, interrogating decisions, and ensuring self-critical analysis. Chapter 1 underscores the importance of humility and openness to self-critique. To be strategic listeners, organizations must seek to locate their own weaknesses and failures. To assess the degree to which these principles are supported in the organization, appraisers should aim to discover the following:

- Are unit or organizational representatives listening with vulnerability and a willingness to withhold defensiveness?
- Is there an eagerness to engage with what is gathered through listening?
- Is there follow-up and investment in an ongoing listening endeavor to a wide array of stakeholders to garner a variety of perspectives?

It is also important to appraise the degree to which a unit or organization understands, supports, and promotes listening ethics. As numerous examples in previous chapters have highlighted, ethics is often at the core of effective listening. Ethics of listening involves thoughtful decision-making, monitoring, and oversight of the manner of listening; the treatment of those who are heard; and the consideration of the content of what listeners hear. Appraisers will want to learn what ethical principles are applied to listening activities, including the following:

- Who should or should not be listened to?
- Under what circumstances may listening occur (especially sensitive topics)?
- Who may have access to what is heard? And what responsibilities do they have regarding confidentiality?
- Is covert listening practiced and endorsed? Who may approve?
- May units or organizations engage in competitive intelligence gathering? How is this activity monitored, and what limits are put on this activity?
- How are ideals of respect for privacy included in listening practices?
- Should everyone (no matter what motivations) be listened to?
- Should those who are listened to be given equal credit?
- And what are the ethics surrounding discrediting those who speak?

Resources that support listening. As the appraisal team members work to assess the activities and principles of listening, they will also need to consider what systems, channels, staff, budget, technology, policies, time, and attention are in place to support listening in the unit or organization. Most valuable activities in organizations need significant investment of resources to be effective. The appraisers will want to determine the degree to which a unit or organization has the necessary infrastructure and resources dedicated to listening activities and processes. Chapter 1 introduced the importance of a wide aperture for listening, noting that organizations need to determine the appropriate strategic aperture to enable them to hear from a variety of useful and diverse sources without overwhelming their processing system. It is possible that an underresourced listening function or role could easily be overwhelmed by increasing input and information, which may lead to confusion when encountering conflicting input and gridlock when information-gathering units do not have the appropriate direction in filtering or limiting what is collected. Appraisers should seek to understand the following:

- What are the number, range, and typical use of listening structures and processes?
- Which structures and processes are used for what purposes and stakeholders?
- Is listening specialized and focused in the unit or organization, or is there a need for all staff to be involved in all sorts of listening activity?
- Are there challenges in coordinating what different parts of the unit or organization are learning through the listening activity?

- To what extent do staff who monitor listening channels feel overwhelmed?
- Are there strategies and practices in place to cope with information overload?
- What are the consequences, if any, of overload?
- Are there efficient processes and technologies in use to support listening?
- Are there important unmet resource needs for those tasked with listening?
- Is there sufficient training for staff and units in information processing and listening?

Approaches to listening. As an appraisal process unfolds, it will be important to gain an understanding of the processes and approaches that are utilized to listen to stakeholders. In the introduction to this book, examples of Cassandras who were ignored or whose warnings were downplayed were often cases of systemic or ongoing failures to listen, rather than mere incidents of poor listening. As these cases help highlight, it is critical to discover the routine ways in which units and organizations listen. The appraisal team should work to understand the following:

- To what degree is a listening activity planned and scheduled?
- Is listening treated as a "nice-to-have" activity or a core activity?
- Are there organizational "dashboard" indicators that help decision-makers determine whether listening is being done well on a routine basis?
- Is there a consistent effort to build listening processes and activities into all new major initiatives and programs?
- What are routine listening activities, and what are the means used to compel them?
- Is listening considered a generous and spontaneous act or a required part of performing tasks and jobs?
- Is routine quality listening expected, rewarded, and supported in the organization?

Insight gained through listening. As I argued in the opening chapters of this book, strategic listening requires that the unit or organization not only permit stakeholders to express ideas, concerns, questions, feedback, and input but also to devote resources to the interpretation, consideration, and analysis of what is heard. In appraising the strategic listening of a unit or organization, thought should be given to how to assess the ways in which what is heard is used. Decision-makers and leaders will need to know what they need to know, set up systems and structures to collect that input, and then channel what is heard back into decisions. The appraisal team will want to explore with decision-makers how they use and interpret information, perspectives, and concerns that are collected. In addition, it is important to assess the barriers and challenges in moving input from stakeholders toward decision-makers. Appraisers should ask questions such as the following:

- What routines are in place to ensure that concerning feedback, input, and bad news are moved up the chain to decision-makers?
- What methods are used by decision-makers to ensure that they have access to the complete spectrum of perspectives (including those that are disconfirming)?
- Is some information or input left unanalyzed? Why?
- Are there sources of input that are routinely considered suspicious or unreliable? Why?
- What do decision-makers not hear that they need to hear?
- As decision-makers review input, what methods do they use to organize, review, and analyze it?
- Is input gained through listening activities considered important to decisions? If not, why not?

Satisfaction of stakeholders with listening. The focus of this book is on strategic benefits of listening to the unit or organization; thus, less attention has been paid to the stakeholders' perspectives in being heard. However, even when adopting a strategic focus in designing listening processes and activities, organizations must be mindful of how stakeholders perceive the listening that is occurring. If stakeholders perceive that their suggestions, objections, concerns, or ideas are routinely ignored, they will be discouraged from continuing to offer them. Further, if stakeholders perceive that listening is inauthentic, weak, poorly executed, or absent, they are providing a clue to a listening failure. The appraisal team should make efforts to assess the following:

- How satisfied are stakeholders with the quality of the listening activity overall?
- Is there variation in views and perspectives? In what ways?
- When has listening worked very well in this organization? When has it failed?
- Does listening simply focus on the most demanding stakeholders?
- Do employees feel that they can upwardly communicate their issues and concerns without fear of retaliation?

Espoused values related to listening. The quality of listening is a product of habits, resources, infrastructure, and leadership. At a fundamental level, listening is determined by the value that is placed on it by the unit or organization. If it is viewed as a nice-to-have rather than a critical function, it is less likely to be routinely carried out in careful and meaningful ways. An important area for the appraisal team to explore is the degree to which the unit or organization espouses the value of listening. That is, do the organization's leaders, human resources staff, customer/client services managers, and other key managers talk about the importance of listening on a routine basis? Key topics to explore in the appraisal process include the following:

- Is listening implicated in the mission, values, and culture of the unit or organization? In what ways?
- Is "listening" called out in any key statement, document, or internal or external communication? How is it portrayed (as a privilege, a duty, an expectation, or an opportunity to learn)?
- Is the importance of listening to fellow employees underscored during training and onboarding?
- Is the importance of listening to clients/customers underscored to staff who provide direct contact or service?
- Are employees told that their voices matter, and are they encouraged to speak up when they have input to provide (no matter whether it is critical or supportive of current decisions)?
- Are clients/customers told that their ideas, suggestions, concerns, and questions are important?

CONCLUSION

A comprehensive appraisal of an organization's listening would be a significant undertaking that would require time, effort, planning, and intentional goal setting. The audience and the goals for the listening appraisal data and analysis should be identified before collecting data. Any unit or organization could certainly undertake a more focused appraisal of part of its listening activities, infrastructure, and culture. A more focused approach could be accomplished in a relatively short time with minimal investment of resources.

It will be important for organizations to keep up with a continual monitoring of listening once an initial appraisal has been conducted. To ensure that listening continues to be strategic, robust, and healthy, organizations should devise a means to periodically benchmark their listening. Repeating questionnaires, conducting a handful of interviews, or periodically raising listening as a topic of review in meetings is a good practice for continuing the benchmarking process.

REFERENCE

Patton, M. Q. (1982). *Practical evaluation*. Beverly Hills, CA: Sage Publications.

Chapter Seven

Building and Maintaining Strategic Listening

This concluding chapter will focus on practical ways that teams, departments, units, or whole organizations can strengthen their listening routines, practices, and culture. The chapter provides a planning framework to improve an organization's strategic listening. The creation or adjustment of listening practices and resources in a unit or organization should be guided by the appraisal process described in chapter 6. A careful examination of the current practices, resources, roles, and routines will yield insights that can direct the design of new or improved processes and activities. While there is no single best recipe for organizational listening, this chapter provides examples of tools, techniques, interventions, and best practices that may be useful and could be considered by any organization looking for options. This chapter addresses three general areas for building and maintaining strategic listening: culture, infrastructure, and routines and practices. See appendix D for a planning worksheet to aid in methodically developing steps and strategies for building and maintaining a strategic listening focus in your organization.

BUILDING A CULTURE FOR STRATEGIC LISTENING

For an organization to fully invest in a strategic listening focus, leaders and internal stakeholders will need to embrace the values, goals, and identity that goes along with authentic, ethical, and purpose-driven listening. Many of the arguments presented in the earlier chapters of this book serve as a foundation for an organizational culture that values listening. Cultural change is necessary to build an organization that has spontaneous and pervasive reflexes to listen to learn, provide self-critical analysis, and correct decisions. In the introduction to this book, four principles of strategic listening are presented that can serve as a foundation for a strategic listening culture. Leaders will need to infuse their organizations with these principles and support them through a variety of changes that make them real (see Box 7.1).

BOX 7.1:
FOUNDATIONAL PRINCIPLES
OF A STRATEGIC LISTENING CULTURE

Principle 1: Listening is not a gift to those who are listened to; it is a strategic practice for those who listen.

Principle 2: Listening effectively, continuously, and strategically is a requirement for organizational survival and the most important ingredient in achieving goal success.

Principle 3: Strategic organizational listening requires attention to systems, processes, and structures that are designed with purpose to gather data, information, and perspectives and to build knowledge.

Principle 4: Strategic organizational listening is best accomplished through analysis of listening capabilities and areas of inattention; strategically building meaningful listening systems, structures, and processes; and instilling a culture of high-capacity listening among all layers of the organization.

Building a strategic listening culture should be the top priority for transforming organizations from deficient to efficient models of listening, which are discussed in the book's introduction. Establishing a culture of strategic listening will provide a foundation on which other steps of technique, practice, systems, and roles can be built. Organizations that endeavor to build a strategic listening culture should target changes in three areas:

• Leading cultural change
• Establishing and reinforcing listening values and ethics
• Employing consistent and pervasive focus and reinforcement

Leaders will need to embrace, internalize, and model a strategic focus on listening. Key beliefs and taken-for-granted assumptions that often go unarticulated in organizations are at the core of organizational culture. Leaders may not express what they truly believe about the value of employee input, the accuracy of clients'/customers' perspectives, the motivations of organizational critics, the wisdom of community members, or the necessity to monitor environments intensely. To understand the core of the current organizational culture, these beliefs and assumptions will need to be surfaced. To introduce a focus on strategic listening to the organization's culture, leaders will need to consider realignment of their own assumptions and beliefs about listening. This is, of course, much easier to accomplish when there is an authentic buy-in from the highest-level leaders in the organization. Leaders who are unconvinced of the arguments presented in the earlier chapters of this book will likely not embrace other recommendations or model effective and strategic listening.

To start a conversation about the risks of listening failures and the strategic advantages of powerful listening, leaders should be introduced to examples that they respect; statistics and analyses that demonstrate realistic risks of poor listening; and core dashboard indicators that are affected by listening activities, processes, and investments. It will be important for leaders who sincerely buy in to a strategic listening focus to begin to publicly espouse those values, learn to overtly model the associated behaviors, and reward those in middle-level management for doing the same. Oftentimes, behaviors that leaders at the very top of organizations publicly execute will be emulated by those who aspire to climb the leadership ladder.

For example, leaders who doggedly seek out critical input and discourage blind loyalty to their own ideas will send a signal that there is genuine interest in identifying potential weaknesses, missed warnings, and better potential alternatives. Oftentimes, leaders who wish to garner candor from those who are in less powerful positions will move toward collection of anonymous input. However, the danger of this approach is that it may signal to those employees that there is some risk associated with identifying themselves as critics of ideas or decisions made at the top of the organization. If the boss thinks employees need to be protected through anonymity, he or she is implying that critical input is somewhat risky. A far more positive approach to encouraging critical input and candor that signals a culture of openness and directness and a comprehensive evaluation of options and decisions would be to reward those employees who identify problems, concerns, weaknesses, and potential risks. Leaders may reward employees who challenge flawed ideas through praise, positive attention, and further empowering them to develop their thoughts and evidence in more detailed ways (e.g., investigating alternatives, running a trial or pilot test, or gathering further data). It is important for these rewards to be genuine and public (see Box 7.2).

BOX 7.2:
LEADERSHIP TECHNIQUE: CRITICAL CONVERSATIONS

A technique to begin to build a leadership style that supports candor and critical feedback is to host at least one meeting about every major proposal, decision, or plan that bans supportive talk. For the whole of one meeting, the leader directs all those present to only make comments of critique, concern, potential downsides, identification of risks, "what ifs," and other negative content. Everyone in the meeting should be required to participate and those who identify unique, unknown, and previously undiscussed issues and potential problems should be praised and encouraged to elaborate. These *critical conversations*, once normalized, can provide cover for anyone who has second thoughts, reservations, or unsurfaced concerning data, to come forward. It is also important for managers throughout the organization to adopt processes of discussion and decision-making that encourage open, candid, and rigorous exchanges about decisions. Managers that surface previous unknown concerns, potential problems, previously unidentified risks from their own staff should be rewarded for modeling rigor and detailed analyses. As leaders support and encourage managers throughout the organization to support these behaviors, they will help establish a culture that discourages self-censorship, silencing of dissent, and dysfunctional patterns of negating or punishing those who criticize leaders' ideas and plans.

In some organizations, independent teams are created just to serve in a devil's advocate role. Red teams have been used to challenge assumptions, present alternative perspectives, and expose vulnerabilities. Red teams have long been used in military and security contractors and governmental agencies, including the CIA. Businesses and governmental agencies have used red teams to simulate attacks and hacks on systems and develop defenses against identified weaknesses. Any organization could use this technique to normalize the practice of running through downsides and weaknesses in the decisions being made.

Building a culture that values listening and promotes healthy ethics surrounding listening activity will necessitate a stable pattern of rewarding proactive ethical practice as well as discouraging or punishing those who fail to listen or promote unethical practices. Ethics of listening span several critical areas that have been addressed in earlier chapters, including the following:

- Receiving and responding to reports of wrongdoing
- Protecting employees from toxic communication
- Setting and enforcing standards for privacy
- Setting and enforcing standards for competitive intelligence
- Creating and promoting an environment for candor and critique
- Creating and promoting an environment for challenging bias

Many best practices exist to address these ethics considerations. Basic principles for addressing any ethical challenge will include setting standards and expectations, protecting vulnerable persons, following transparent processes, and holding violators accountable. Perhaps the most important best practice for any ethics policy is thorough, consistent communication. No ethical standard will be followed if communication about it is poor. As new employees are onboarded into organizations, they need to be made aware of ethical standards for listening (see Box 7.3). They should be reminded of ethical responsibilities to other stakeholders. Values that underscore ethical standards should also be included in training and made a part of employee performance evaluations.

BOX 7.3:
ETHICS COMMUNICATION BEST PRACTICE:
ADD ETHICS TO ONBOARDING, KEY
STATEMENTS, AND EVALUATION CRITERIA

Key documents, statements, and evaluation criteria should be reviewed as a major step toward remaking the listening culture. Existing messages about the importance and ethics of listening should be revised to adhere to the new cultural focus, and new messages that are necessary for addressing that focus should be added. Important documents and statements to review include job descriptions, offer letters, employee handbooks, mission and value statements, training materials, performance evaluation criteria, external documents, websites, social media statements that pertain to how the organization values its stakeholders, and policy documents (especially those pertaining to reporting wrongdoing).

Cultural change will require consistent and pervasive reinforcement. Rewards and punishments may be a part of the methods to reinforce desired behavior; however, the best practice for accomplishing cultural change often involves repeating desired themes and understandings as well as consistent modeling of desired behavior. Consistency is extremely important for main-taining a culture change. Hypocrisy in leaders' words and behavior will be easily detected. Lingering old culture practices, language, or policies will quickly undermine new culture values, which may then appear to be disin-genuous (see Box 7.4).

BOX 7.4:
CULTURE CHANGE TECHNIQUE:
LEADERS BEING HELD ACCOUNTABLE

QBE Insurance has spent the past few years restructuring its business while also weaving into the fabric of its global organization a strong, cohesive culture. In the process of implementing the cultural change, the CEO, Pat Regan, aimed to become the premier role model for the QBE DNA program's cultural attributes, which were rolled out earlier in 2018. He said, "If I'm not role modeling the [cultural attributes], we've got zero chance of creating it" (para. 6). The cultural change was rolled out with seven key principles, described in terms of a set of hashtags: "1. We are customer-centered (#OutsideIn); 2. We are techni-cal experts (#KnowYourStuff); 3. We are diverse (#MixItUp); 4. We are fast-paced (#RampItUp); 5. We are courageous (#DoTheRightTh-ing); 6. We are accountable (#OwnItNow); and 7. We are a team (#To-gether)" (sidebar).

> Regan aims to create a corporate environment where his colleagues feel comfortable (courageous) enough to tell him when he's not role model-ing the QBE DNA and he's comfortable (courageous) enough to hear it. During the summer, he filmed a video asking people to call him out when he's not role modeling the cultures.
> "It's easy for me to tell people when they're not living the culture, isn't it? But I also need to be aware when I'm not role modeling them. And in the moments when I'm not, people need to tell me. If I can do that, then my team can do that, and their teams can do that. Then we'll be able to create something special," [Regan] emphasized. (para. 9, 10)

Adapted from Howard, L. S. (2019, February 12). A CEO needs to paint a picture of what "good" looks like: QBE CEO Regan. Retrieved from https://www.insurancejournal.com/news/interna-tional/2019/02/12/516947.htm

Researchers Armenakis and Harris (2009) have established that a successful initial rollout of change is more likely when stakeholders hold these five key beliefs:

- There is a need for change.
- This specific change is the best of the alternatives.
- The organization is capable of making this change.
- There is support among organizational leaders for this change.
- This change is good for me personally.

An extensive body of research supports the practice of "creating readiness for change rather than waiting to reduce resistance" (Armenakis & Harris, 2009, p. 129). Further, research supports early communication with stakeholders to help build a rationale for change and an understanding of the best alternatives to implement a change (Lewis, 2019). Applying these arguments to establishment of a new culture of strategic listening, organizations should work to engage stakeholders about the need for improving listening as well as the gaps in current listening activity, process, policy, and values in the organization. Clearly, involvement of a wide set of stakeholders with a robust appraisal process, such as that discussed in the previous chapter, would be an ideal approach to helping to build the key beliefs (see Box 7.5).

BOX 7.5:
CULTURE CHANGE TECHNIQUE:
BUILDING BELIEFS TO SUPPORT CULTURAL CHANGE

Involvement of a wide array of stakeholders in the appraisal process is an excellent way to build the belief that change is necessary and to specifically identify preferred ways to make changes in the organization. As individuals engage in the exploration of current practices, failure events, and weaknesses in listening habits and routines, they will begin to convince themselves of the need to change. Participating in discussion about what it would take to change the organization's culture and developing ideas about how to go about it can increase beliefs that the organization is capable and that there is significant support for change.

A beginning to getting to needed cultural change is wide participation in examination of the current listening problems, activities, infrastructure, processes, and values and then working to make sense with stakeholders about what needs to be changed.

Beyond the first step, a rollout of a cultural change will require setting clear expectations for employees; rewarding behavior that is desirable and consistent with the new culture; and supporting individuals, teams, and units in implementing new activities, processes, and policies. All stakeholders who are affected by a cultural change such as this will need to be folded in to the process of change. I've devoted significant attention to the topic of organizational change in another book (Lewis, 2019); foundational takeaways from that work include the following:

- Knowing your stakeholders' values, needs, and perspectives
- Appreciating the size, scope, controversy, and overall context of the change being introduced
- Understanding the network of stakeholders and how they will influence each other and their responses to this change
- Thorough consideration of the best way to message about the change and how the change will be framed by others
- Development of robust methods of soliciting input from stakeholders about the change and the methods and manner of implementation
- Creating strong support in the organization that enables progress to be made in activating the change, monitoring the change process, and assessing change outcomes

BUILDING STRATEGIC LISTENING INFRASTRUCTURE

A strategic listening infrastructure enables strategic listening. To do listening well, an organization must value it and be willing to engage in listening. However, to be enabled to listen to multiple stakeholders; effectively monitor a multitude of environmental indicators, trends, threats, and opportunities; and analyze and make use of what is learned, an infrastructure needs to be built and maintained. As organizations work toward development of a strategic listening infrastructure, they need to consider a number of critical areas:

- Channels for taking input and active monitoring
- Technologies for listening
- Roles and processes for strategic listening, analysis, and dissemination
- Ongoing evaluation of listening

There are numerous interventions that may be used to enhance and build listening infrastructure, and the results of a thorough appraisal process should yield insights as to which of them are needed in any organization. Channels and technologies may be adopted to augment listening practice in an orga-nization (either internally or with external stakeholders). Like any organi-zational change, they will need to be carefully considered, hopefully, with wide input and introduced with a thoughtful and strategic process. Merely purchasing systems and compelling their use or inviting external stakeholders to embrace their use is unlikely to yield the desired outcomes.

Effective new channels and technologies to assist strategic listening will need to have clear purpose, be well monitored, and enable listening that is not being accomplished in other available ways. As new channels are introduced, it will be important to make clear the value they offer. Stakeholders who have felt ignored or discouraged from speaking will not likely trust a new channel until they see evidence that its use is producing different and positive results.

New technologies and channels should be designed in ways to address a particular need or resolve a particular problem. The implementation of "gen-eral listening" channels is unlikely to meet a particular need. For example, if the need is for the organization to gather reports of problems or concerns that are considered risky to the individual to communicate, an open channel, such as an open-door policy of managers, is unlikely to be used.

The US Federal Aviation Administration (FAA) provides one example of a channel to address the needs for upward communication of risk or problems where there may be a perceived need for anonymity. The FAA has an incident reporting system for pilots to anonymously report problems with an aircraft without their employer or other stakeholders being able to identify them. This channel proved quite important in the recent controversy over the Boeing 737 Max 8 aircraft (two of which were recently involved in fatal crashes that appear to be connected to a common cause). According to *Politico* (Wolfe, 2019), in November 2018, a commercial airline pilot reported that during takeoff the autopilot was engaged and "'within two to three seconds the aircraft pitched nose down' in a manner steep enough to trigger the plane's warning system, which sounded 'Don't sink, don't sink!'" (para. 3). In both of the recent crashes, the planes also descended sharply more than once as pilots wrestled with the controls before crashing. In the case of Lion Air, pre-liminary facts suggest that the cause may have been the antistall system. The *Politico* article describes other complaints by pilots in this incident database related to the Boeing aircraft and the lack of appropriate response to concerns, including the following:

> While the FAA had issued an emergency directive on Nov. 7, 2018, to help pi-lots understand how to handle problems with the anti-stall technology, "it does nothing to address the systems issues," the pilot wrote. The pilot further noted that the flight manuals had yet to be updated with that information at that time.

"I think it is unconscionable that a manufacturer, the FAA, and the airlines would have pilots flying an airplane without adequately training, or even providing available resources and sufficient documentation to understand the highly complex systems that differentiate this aircraft from prior models," the pilot wrote. (para. 11, 12)

The online anonymous incident database is clearly providing a platform for pilots fearing retribution from their own employers (or other stakeholders) to provide critically needed information in this public safety crisis. However, it appears that repeated reporting did not initially result in the intended effect of motivating the FAA, Boeing, or the airlines to take action (although the Trump administration did eventually order the grounding of the 737 Max 8 and Max 9 aircrafts). Although an anonymous channel may be appropriate for this situation, this example also clearly underscores one key disadvantage of such systems—there is no way to follow up and garner more details or interview those who made the reports.

Another listening technology serves as an example of a creative means to provide citizens a voice in city planning. Community PlanIt is an online game platform that encourages deliberation and civic participation as citizens get to "play" with ideas for their city. The tool was created by the Engagement Lab (n.d.) at Emerson College, an applied research and design lab that investigates technology and media for civic participation. It describes this tool as follows:

Within a series of time-limited missions, players compete with each other to earn influence in their community to fund local projects. At the same time, they learn about key issues related to the topic of the engagement process, connect with each other, and suggest solutions to problems. Each game culminates in a face-to-face community event, where players meet with each other and discuss the results of the process and next steps with curators of the game and other decision makers. (para. 3)

The tool is intended to short-circuit many of the typical problems with open town hall and community meetings, which can often be marked by lack of diversity, learning, and trust and an overabundance of one-issue activists, incivility, and misunderstandings. Community PlanIt allows cities and organizations to guide constituents through the narrative of the planning process, creating opportunities along the way for learning, civil conversation, and meaningful input. According to the Engagement Lab website, the game has been played by over 10,000 people across a dozen cities and has been used in a wide array of contexts, including public health prioritization, waste-water management, social media policy, and youth unemployment.

Of course, technologies and channels for listening will only be as effective as the individuals who staff them. Unattended or poorly monitored channels will not yield benefit to those who use them or to the organization or unit sponsoring them. Organizations will need to also build infrastructure in terms of creating roles and processes for listening, analysis, and dissemination. Critical roles that could be dedicated to listening functions or be a part of another position include the following:

- Information and knowledge workers to search for, collect, curate, evaluate, organize, and disseminate information
- Facilitators who can design and manage group discussions, meetings, and input-seeking gatherings as well as serve in collaborative partnerships as process experts
- Competitive intelligence experts who have training and expertise in ethical and legal means of gathering needed information about competitors
- Ombudspersons who are provided independence in taking and evaluating reports of wrongdoing and concerns about listening activity in the organization (either the lack of it or toxic examples)
- Listening trainers who are tasked with improving the overall listening techniques and capabilities of individual employees and whole units (from increasing diversity engagement; to helping managers learn to listen more carefully to their frontline employees; to improving evaluation of scientific and technical evidence, discerning information needs, and assisting in identifying subjects to be listened to)

Individuals asked to take on new roles or expand their current roles to include these listening-related competencies will likely need training, mentoring, and opportunities to develop their roles. Introducing these new responsibilities and roles in organizations will follow a process similar to that for more general cultural change. The individuals tasked with these functions should be led through the evidence that builds the case for the need for change and support for this approach to the change in the organization. They will also need to be given resources to support their new role. This may involve additional training, staff, budget, and consultant help to initiate programs.

The ombudsperson is one example of a key role that many organizations now use to enhance listening. According to the International Ombudsman Association (IOA, n.d.) website, an ombudsman/person:

> is one who assists individuals and groups in the resolution of conflicts or concerns. There are a number of different titles or names for this position: "ombudsman," "ombudsperson" or "ombuds" among others. . . . Ombudsmen work in all types of organizations, including government agencies, colleges and universities, corporations, hospitals and other medical facilities, and news organizations. . . . The organizational ombudsman is defined as: "a designated neutral who is appointed or employed by an organization to facilitate the informal resolution

of concerns of employees, managers, students and, sometimes, external clients of the organization." (para. 1, 3)

An ombudsperson is above all else a listener and a conduit of learning. According to the IOA, the most important skills of an effective ombudsperson are active listening, communication with a diverse range of people, remaining nonjudgmental, speaking up to higher levels within an organization, problem solving, and conflict resolution skills. Many of these same skills are a part of the other roles called out in the above list.

To maintain a strong listening infrastructure in the organization, leaders will need to ensure that there is ongoing evaluation and adjustment to listening systems, processes, policies, and resources. One of the best ways to assess the effectiveness of the changes in the listening infrastructure is to repeat, at some level, the appraisal process described in chapter 6. If a short version of the appraisal can be collected on a periodic basis, the organization can benchmark its listening outcomes and continue to track them over time.

BUILDING STRATEGIC LISTENING ROUTINES AND PRACTICES

As organizations undergo a process to build a strategic listening culture, it will be critical for them to envision a new culture; communicate new values, mission, and ethics; and create new channels, technologies, and roles. However, the most consequential component to bring this new culture to life is the alteration of routines and practices of listening. Best practices for strategic listening practice should be constructed around the following key areas:

- Regular daily routines
- Guidelines for unexpected events and crises
- Protocols for evaluation of warnings
- Creating a listening dashboard

In developing new routines for regular, daily practice, it will be very important to provide individuals, groups, and those in key communication roles with rubrics, templates, models, and reminders of how to perform new listening activities. As individuals learn new ways to communicate and break old habits, they will need these kinds of tools. Once strategic listening becomes a natural part of routines, fewer aids to reinforce these behaviors will be necessary. A full scaffolding of new skills and practice would involve training, role-playing and drilling, support materials, follow-up with trainers or supervisors, and retraining as necessary (see Box 7.6).

BOX 7.6:
TECHNIQUE FOR BUILDING NEW
HABITS OF LISTENING: SCAFFOLDING

To prompt employees to master new skills, behaviors, routines, and habits, training is an essential place to begin. It is important to provide people new to listening skills the opportunity to practice what they are learning in role-plays or other simulations. As individuals gain hands-on practice with new skills and practices, they will learn not only what the organization wants from them but also what they currently don't fully understand about the practices. They will encounter scenarios and nuances that test their comprehension of the desired outcome and that will further push trainers to detail how to handle new situations and circumstances.

Once trainees begin to practice new skills and routines on the job, they will need support in the form of templates, reminders, rubrics, and scripts. These tools can help them to recall how to handle specific situations and provide them with options. Those newly assigned to strategic listening tasks might need materials and resources to plan meetings, run input sessions, take customer/client complaints, review social media postings about the organization, and evaluate satisfaction survey results, among many other possibilities.

After trainees have an opportunity to practice their new tasks and skills in their jobs, it is important to provide contact with mentors, trainers, and supervisors who can check in with them about unresolved questions or needs for further training.

As organizations become more fluent in strategic listening in daily routines, they run the risk of normalizing their practices to the point that they will not recognize the need for added attention or new approaches in the context of significant unexpected events and crises. At a time of crises or major unique events, organizations will often need to reassess their standards for practices of listening. More listening or different approaches to listening are often necessary during crises.

The current crisis of measles outbreak in the United States offers a current example of the need to adapt listening strategies. As the antivax movement in the United States has grown, the risk of a resurgence of the once-defeated disease has grown. In New York City, Mayor de Blasio ordered mandatory vaccinations for some Brooklyn neighborhoods. A massive campaign to increase vaccination rates has yielded less success than hoped, "despite the

30,000 robocalls and hundreds of fliers from the city, urging, cajoling and threatening parents to vaccinate their children or face fines—the distrust of government and concern that vaccines do more harm than good is forming a significant roadblock to city officials' efforts to slow the outbreak's progress" (Nahmias, Goldberg, & Eisenberg, 2019, para 22).

One possible reason for the challenges experienced in New York and elsewhere is illustrated by a former antivaxxer, Christine Vigeant, who told her story of change to *USA Today* (Dastigir, 2019). She explains that efforts to argue her views were never persuasive. Vigeant said that, when people tried to counter her beliefs with facts, it only made her more resolute and made her feel as though she was being ridiculed. "We're called bad parents. That drives people away. It doesn't make them feel that their concerns are being heard, and it makes them retreat right back into that echo chamber" (Dastigir, 2019, para. 19). Vigeant eventually came around to a perspective supporting vaccination through a gentle and respectful set of conversations with people she trusts. She now says,

> "When I approach people now who hold beliefs that I used to hold myself, I try to start by asking questions. I ask them why they believe what they believe. I try to better understand them before giving my thoughts," she said. "These people care very much for their children, they just have very different ideas of what it means to do that." (Dastigir, 2019, para. 44)

Conducting *after-action reviews* (AARs) is one best practice for learning from crises. AARs are a common practice in the military. They are often used as an ongoing practice throughout an extended period of action. That is, it is not a single meeting, report, or conversation but many. According to a 2005 article (Darling, Parry, & Moore, 2005) in the *Harvard Business Review* on AARs in a business context,

> The reference to AAR *meetings*—plural—is important. While a corporate team might conduct one AAR meeting at the end of a six-month project, OPFOR [the military version] holds dozens of AARs at different levels in a single week. Each unit holds an AAR meeting immediately after each significant phase of an action. If time is short, such meetings may be no more than ten-minute huddles around the hood of a Humvee. (para. 23)

Organizations can routinize the examination of major events and crisis communication to evaluate what could have been done better and what was learned and, most importantly, do so in an ongoing pattern of continuous evaluation and adjustment.

Organizations should also consider developing protocols for evaluation of received warnings. As the examples earlier in this book illustrate, Cassandra warnings may arrive at any time. The attention and serious consideration warnings receive can easily determine much about the level and appropriateness of response and the potential for a damaging or even catastrophic outcome. In the case of warnings, an after-listening reflection can be a useful tool (see Box 7.7).

BOX 7.7:
TECHNIQUE FOR BUILDING ROUTINES:
AFTER-LISTENING REFLECTION

In executing an after-listening reflection, organizational leaders should pose important critical questions, such as

- What have we heard?
- What have we learned?
- What actions will we take as a result?

It is critical that these questions be considered in proactive, authentic, and serious ways. When organizations receive a warning that, if true, could be devastating or alarming or represent an extreme risk, there must be an equal level of serious examination of what is heard. Hearing a Cassandra's warning is not the same as accepting or believing it. However, thorough and authentic listening is critical in high-risk situations.

As leaders consider what has been heard and what has been learned, active steps will need to be taken to avoid the traps identified in the book Warnings: Finding Cassandras to Stop Catastrophes (Clarke & Eddy, 2017) and described in the opening chapters of this book. It is common and easy for leaders to dismiss unlikely events, develop strong group norms to protect a sense of infallibility, disregard unique information or evidence, demand perfect data, and resist information and perspectives that force the questioning of leaders. To be diligent in an after-listening reflection, leaders will need to be aware of these dynamics and strive for vigilant examination of potential threats and risks.

To support healthy listening practices and routines in an organization, leaders should create and occasionally update a *listening dashboard*. A strategic dashboard is a reporting tool that organizations use to monitor critical success factors. High-level leaders of a unit or an organization will turn to these analytics to determine whether the organizational strategy is on target to reach goals. A listening dashboard does the same thing in the domain of listening. Creating a listening dashboard involves thinking about the major analytics, metrics, and critical data that can be routinely gathered, reported, and followed to determine the success the organization is having with executing its strategic organizational listening goals. A particularly powerful dashboard will provide a quick visual representation of the overall health of the strategic listening activity in the organization (see Box 7.8).

BOX 7.8:
LISTENING DASHBOARD ELEMENTS

Indicators of listening skills acquired and support for listening by employees

Number of employees having completed training
Number of employees having achieved high-level mastery of skills
Level of routine use of best practices for listening across contexts
Level of self-confidence in listening skills and infrastructure to support
    listening

Indicators of quality listening activity

Level or frequency of outreach and input gathering
Frequency of repeat participants in input-gathering sessions and activities
Level or frequency of use of new channels or technologies for providing input
Level of reported satisfaction of critical stakeholders with listening

Indicators of quality internal processing of what is heard through listening activity

Speed of processing input and dissemination to decision-makers
Satisfaction of decision-makers in acquiring needed input and perspectives

Indicators of new learning

Quality of new ideas and suggestions surfaced
Level of insight gathered into previously unidentified issues and concerns
Regularity of new learning that has been acquired about environment
Regularity of new perspectives shared in internal decision-making

Tracking a strategic listening dashboard may be a challenging undertaking for many organizations. The key principles of strategic organizational listening require that organizations aim to learn from their listening activity, not merely engage in listening. An ideal dashboard would capture what is newly discovered and what influence these discoveries have on decision-making. However, metrics to assess these impacts are often more qualitative than easily indexed data of other types (e.g., sales, participation rates in programs, and social media mentions). Organizational leaders will have to be creative in determining what to track in their own organizations that will reflect the connections between authentic, strategic listening activity and the influence of what is heard on learning, self-critical analysis, and questioning of assumptions and decisions.

CONCLUSION

This chapter has provided a framework for building and maintaining a strategic listening focus. Although any effective effort to continuously build and improve listening in an organization will necessitate creativity and individually adapted approaches, the elements presented here are strong points of departure. Organizations aiming to improve or further the strength of strategic listening should focus on culture, infrastructure, and routines and practices. These three categories reflect attention to listening values, support, and processes. Investment and monitoring of all three are a strong basis for keeping organizational strategic listening on track.

Organizational listening failures may lead to financial ruin, legal jeopardy, and reputational crises and bring harm to stakeholder relationships and to stakeholders themselves. Effective and strategic organizational listening ensures that an organization's attention is directed toward vital information and input to enable learning, questioning of key assumptions, interrogating decisions, and ensuring self-critical analysis. Organizations have for a very long time undervalued the power of strategic listening. That power can be strategically harnessed through careful and strategic application of listening practices, techniques, and processes and consistent listening leadership.

REFERENCES

Armenakis, A. A., & Harris, S. G. (2009). Reflections: Our journey in organizational change research and practice. *Journal of Change Management*, *9*(2), 127–142.

Clarke, R. A., & Eddy, R. P. (2017). *Warnings: Finding Cassandras to stop catastrophes*. New York, NY: HarperCollins.

Darling, M., Parry, C., & Moore, J. (2005, July–August). Learning in the thick of it. *Harvard Business Review*. Retrieved from https://hbr.org/2005/07/learning-in-the-thick-of-it

Dastigir, A. E. (2019, April 8). Facts alone don't sway anti-vaxxers. So what does? *USA Today*. Retrieved from https://www.usatoday.com/story/news/investigations/2019/03/08/vaccine-anti-vax-anti-vaxxer-what-change-their-mind-vaccine-hesitancy/3100216002/

Engagement Lab. (n.d.). Community PlanIt: Challenge. Retrieved from https://elab.emerson.edu/projects/community-planit

Howard, L. S. (2019, February 12). A CEO needs to paint a picture of what "good" looks like: QBE CEO Regan. Retrieved from https://www.insurancejournal.com/news/international/2019/02/12/516947.htm

International Ombudsman Association. (n.d.). About ombuds: What is an organizational ombudsman? Retrieved from https://www.ombudsassociation.org/what-is-an-organizational-ombuds

Lewis, L. (2019). *Organizational change: Creating change through strategic communication.* (2nd ed.). Chichester, UK: Wiley Blackwell.

Nahmias, L., Goldberg, D., & Eisenberg, A. (2019, April 19). Measles outbreak tests limits of religious freedom in New York City. *Politico*. Retrieved from https://www.politico.com/story/2019/04/15/measles-new-york-1276927

Wolfe, K. A. (2019, March 12). Pilots complained at least 5 times about Boeing 737 Max problems, records show. Retrieved from https://www.politico.com/story/2019/03/12/pilots-boeing-737-1266090?fbclid=IwAR2bfM-CwlETMX7vt-vEzK-ViZuinnzi8HOI1_TJkfwgDPP2EKBeIvMviBo4

ADDITIONAL RESOURCE

Engagement Lab at Emerson College: https://elab.emerson.edu/about

Appendix A

Observational Guide

Ideally, observers will be trained to interpret the following categories in similar ways. This is best done by having the observation team members meet and discuss what each category and comment means and then watch a small set of samples of listening together. They should then individually complete their guide and compare their notes. Discussion of how different observers recorded what they saw and any comments or evaluation that was connected to it will help to calibrate the observation. If many observations are to occur in the organization over a lengthy period, observation team members should reconvene and go through the process of calibration a second or even third time to ensure that there is no "drift" in the way the guide is being applied by different team members.

Observation Location:

Time and Date:

Indicate which of the following listening activities is expected to occur in this setting:

	Intake of complaint
	Intake of inquiry
	Executing customer order, purchase, or transaction
	Executing customer return or exchange
	Interdepartmental coordination
	Soliciting input to decision-making and planning
	Soliciting feedback on program and policy activity
	Soliciting evaluation
	Soliciting concerns
	Soliciting knowledge and insights
	Soliciting report of experience
	Obtaining problem description
	Other

Describe the demeanor of the listener:

Describe the demeanor of the persons being listened to:

Rate the quality of information obtained by the listeners (1 = poor quality, 2 = modest quality, 3 = moderate quality, 4 = somewhat high quality, 5 = high quality):

What makes you give that rating?

Describe the tactics used by the listener to obtain more information, explanation, and details from the person he or she is listening to, and rate how effective he or she seems to be:

Tactic	Effectiveness
Asked direct questions	Example: The person did not understand what was asked; this tactic failed.
Summarized what was heard to confirm accuracy	
Asked for elaboration of a point made; asked whether the person had any more detail to add	
Asked for example of something claimed or shared	
Encouraged speakers to say more, talk more, or engage more	
Made explicit statement of one's desire to hear what the speakers have to say; stated that what is shared has value and importance	
Made explicit statement about how what is heard will be used in decision-making or other processes	
Waited quietly while the speakers formulated their thoughts	

Describe any behaviors that the listener demonstrates that might indicate that he or she is trying to listen carefully and attentively:

Behaviors	Description
Making consistent eye contact	
Taking notes about what is said	
Summarizing what he or she has understood	
Asking clarifying questions	
Giving undivided attention (e.g., no phones, laptops, or clock watching)	
Expressing empathy and appreciation	
Remaining quiet while the speaker is talking	

Describe any indicators that the speaker is satisfied with the listening:

Indicators	Description
Expression of satisfaction and gratitude	
Responsiveness to clarifying questions	
Contribution of elaboration of information when asked	
Continuation with engaging with listener	
Continuous focus on listener	

Appendix B

Interview Guide

Ideally, interviewers will be trained to ask questions; listen closely for responses; take detailed notes; and probe and follow up with prompts for further information, details, and examples. This is best done by having the interview team members meet and discuss what each question is meant to gather and then practice interviewing one another or watch an interview together. They should then individually complete notes and compare what they have recorded. Discussion of how different interviewers recorded their notes will help to calibrate their interview styles.

Tell me about a time when you felt someone in this organization listened to you.
What made you think they were listening to you?
What effect did those things have on you?
Tell me about a time when you felt someone in this organization did not listen to you.
What made you think he or she was not listening to you?
What effect did those things have on you?
What could have been done or said by this organization to better listen to you?
From your observations and experiences, in what ways does this organization value listening?
Why do you say that?
Can you give examples that illustrate what you think?
What do you think are the ways in which this organization listens best?
What do you think are the ways this organization is lacking in listening?
Who gets listened to by this organization most? Who gets listened to least?

How do you know when someone in this organization is really listening to you?

When you are in meetings with others in this organization, how do you know that listening is happening? How do you know when it isn't happening?

What sorts of things external to this organization are often missed because no one is listening for them?

When have individuals external to this organization attempted to be heard but been ignored or discouraged from sharing what they knew or thought?

What is an example of a costly mistake made by this organization related to poor listening?

What is an example of a positive change or wise reversal of a decision made by this organization due to good listening?

Appendix C

Questionnaire Item Bank

QUESTIONS ABOUT ACTIVITIES AND PRACTICES

1. Rate (very ineffective to very effective) each of the following listening-related activities:
   a. Recognizing the need for information
   b. Recognizing the need for accurate and complete information
   c. Formulating questions based on the need for information
   d. Identification of potential sources of information
   e. Development of search strategies for information
   f. Use of computer-based and other technology for information needs
   g. Evaluation of information
   h. Organization of gathered information for application
   i. Integration of information into existing bodies of knowledge
   j. Use of information in critical thinking and problem solving
2. How effective (very ineffective to very effective) are the unit's or organization's routines for each of the following activities:
   a. Collecting critiques, concerns, and dissent
   b. Collecting bad news
   c. Collecting early warnings of problems or negative consequences
   d. Collecting views, perspectives, opinions, and needs
3. Describe the most common method in this unit or organization for listening to the following and state for each method how often it is used:
   a. Questions, critiques, concerns, and dissent
   b. Complaints
   c. Problems and early warning signs of negative consequences
   d. Bad news
   e. Views, perspectives, opinions, and needs

4. Which of the following groups of stakeholders are routinely listened to by this unit or organization:
   a. [Enter in groups of identified relevant stakeholders.]
   b. [Rate each group's level of being heard by the unit.]

QUESTIONS ABOUT PROBLEMS

1. Describe an important listening-related problem that this unit or organization has.
2. How frequently (very rarely to very frequently) does this problem come up?
3. How much harm (very little to very much) to the unit or organization is related to this problem?
4. Which of the following items are worsened by this problem? Check all that apply.
   a. Efficiency of task completion
   b. Effectiveness of job performance
   c. Timeliness of task completion
   d. Employee morale
   e. Employee retention
   f. Customer satisfaction
   g. Customer retention
   h. Coordination among units
   i. Decision-making quality
5. Which of the following attempts have been made to solve this problem?
   a. No attempts that I'm aware of.
   b. Individuals have attempted to address the problem.
   c. A team or unit has taken a detailed approached to address the problem.
   d. A significant organizational effort has been made to address the problem.

QUESTIONS ABOUT PRINCIPLES

1. Indicate the degree to which you agree or disagree (strongly agree to strongly disagree) with each of the following descriptions of this organization's listening principles:
   a. Listening in this organization is an essential part of everything we do.
   b. Listening in this organization is a nice-to-have practice when we have time.

    c. Listening in this organization is intentional and focused.

    d. Listening is emphasized as a core practice.

    e. The importance of careful listening is frequently underscored by leaders.

    f. Leaders in this organization frequently emphasize that we need to listen to each other.

    g. Taking input from external stakeholders is considered an essential step of planning and decision-making.

    h. This organization listens only to what it wants to hear.

    i. Leaders in this organization say that they want to listen, but they are not genuine.

    j. The only time listening is emphasized in this organization is when leadership is talking.

    k. The purpose of listening in this organization is to learn what is not known.

    l. People who are really listened to in this organization are those in power.

    m. This organization is constantly listening to everyone and everything.

    n. This organization encourages us to spy on one another and report what we learn.

    o. If you are considered a problem employee, you will not be listened to.

    p. Complainers do not get listened to in this organization.

2. The essential principle of listening in this organization is:

QUESTIONS ABOUT RESOURCES

1. The most effective support for listening used in this organization is:

2. The most needed resource to improve listening in this organization is:

3. To make listening more effective in this organization, we should invest in:

4. Which of the following problems with enabling listening in this organization are significant? Check all that apply.

    a. Employees feeling overwhelmed with what they are hearing

    b. Limited capacity or method to channel what is heard up the chain

    c. Poor technology for collecting what needs to be listened to

    d. Poor or absent training for employees to collect needed information and input

    e. Poor or absent training for employees to summarize and analyze information and input that is collected

    f. Limited capabilities to share information with units and individuals who need it

QUESTIONS ABOUT APPROACHES

1. Which of the following words (in the pairs) best describe this organization's approach to listening?

   a. Proactive   Reactive
   b. Ethical   Unethical
   c. Disorganized   Organized
   d. Inconsistent   Consistent
   e. Routine   Scattered
   f. Quality   Substandard

2. Which of the following items are on this organization's "listening dashboard" that leaders routinely monitor and care about (indicate not very important to very important):

   a. Adequacy of listening to customers/clients
   b. Adequacy of listening and collecting data about competitors
   c. Adequacy of listening to employees
   d. Adequacy of listening resources, technology, and channels
   e. Adequacy of analysis and circulation of information and insights heard

QUESTIONS ABOUT INSIGHTS GAINED

1. Which of the following words (in the pairs) best describe this organization's routines for analysis of input that is collected through listening:

   a. Adequate   Inadequate
   b. Biased   Unbiased
   c. Scattered   Thorough
   d. Uneven   Reliable
   e. Insightful   Unintelligent
   f. Useless   Useful

2. As you think about how this organization analyzes the input, feedback, and information it collects, rate (not true to very true) each of the following statements:

   a. Input is summarized in useful ways.
   b. Input analysis is provided to decision-makers in a timely way.
   c. Input analysis is relevant to the unit's needs.
   d. Input analysis answers the most important questions units and decision-makers have.
   e. Input analysis is customized to the needs of the unit and decision-makers.
   f. Analysis of information is done in a manner to ensure urgent insights are expedited to decision-makers.

3. When the organization hears "outlier" information and input that does not align with other indicators, how is that information analyzed?

QUESTIONS ABOUT SATISFACTION OF STAKEHOLDERS
QUESTIONNAIRE ITEMS FOR EMPLOYEES

1. Rate the degree to which this organization is good at listening to employees.
2. Rate the degree to which you personally feel listened to by this organization.
3. How satisfied are you with the overall listening that occurs in this organization?
4. Rate the listening quality that occurs in the following contexts in this organization:
   a. Within my work team or group
   b. In meetings with only my peers present
   c. In meetings with my manager(s) present
   d. In one-on-one meetings with my manager(s)
   e. In meetings with high-level leaders
5. Part of healthy listening in organizations is hearing the "hard stuff" (negative comments, complaints, concerns, and bad news).
   a. How well does your organization listen to the hard stuff from within this organization?
   b. How well does this organization listen to the hard stuff from people outside of this organization?
6. If you had something negative or critical to say about this organization, its operation, its decisions, or the implications of its decisions, would you feel comfortable sharing that with your manager? Why or why not?
7. How often (never to frequently) do you keep quiet about a flaw, problem, concern, or brewing issue in this organization because you do not want to be the person to deliver the bad news?

QUESTIONNAIRE ITEMS FOR CLIENTS/CUSTOMERS

1. Rate the degree to which this organization is good at listening to customers/clients.
2. Rate the degree to which you personally feel listened to by this organization.
3. How satisfied are you with the overall listening that occurs by this organization?

4. Rate the listening quality that occurs in the following contexts in this organization:
   a. When receiving services
   b. When raising a problem or concern
   c. When making a suggestion
   d. When asking for clarification or further information
   e. When protesting a decision or practice
5. Describe a time when you felt this organization did not listen to you:
6. Describe a time when you felt this organization listened to you well:

QUESTIONS ABOUT ESPOUSED VALUES

1. To what extent do leaders in this organization talk about the importance of listening?
2. Is listening mentioned in the vision and mission statements of this organization?
3. Is listening part of this organization's training and onboarding of new employees?
4. Are channels of listening described to new employees?
5. Does this organization make it clear to customers/clients that their views, ideas, opinions, and concerns are important?

Appendix D

Planning Framework
for Enhancing Strategic Listening

BUILDING A CULTURE OF STRATEGIC LISTENING

- What is the current need (low, medium, or high) to bring top-level leaders on board with increasing or creating a culture of strategic listening?
- Plan for starting a conversation with top-level leaders about strategic listening in this organization:
  - How will candid conversations surfacing beliefs and taken-for-granted assumptions about how listening should occur and its importance to the organization's significant goals and mission be done?
  - What data, benchmarking, critical incidents, and risk analysis will be presented to leaders to underscore the importance of listening and the weaknesses in listening habits, processes, and infrastructure? The data from the listening appraisal would be ideal for this presentation.
- What new methods will be employed to signal top-level leaders' seriousness about listening in the organization?
  - Which techniques will be used to garner candid input?
  - Which techniques will be used to reward those who provide critique and cautionary information and views?
- What updating needs to be done in listening-related ethics policies, messages, and statements. What is lacking? What is contradictory? What is inconsistent with practice?
- What new messaging needs to be made to new employees related to listening expectations and philosophy?
- What realignments are necessary between job descriptions and performance evaluation criteria related to listening?

- Consider the following questions when planning a rollout for a new cultural emphasis on strategic listening:
  - What strategies will be used to build beliefs that change is needed, change is desirable, change is possible, change is supported, and change is a positive?
  - How can stakeholders be involved in exploring the needs for a cultural change?
  - How can leaders make clear their support for a cultural change in listening?
  - What benefits of strategic listening to various stakeholders can be highlighted?
- What is your organization's plan for implementing a listening culture?
  - What are your stakeholders' values, needs, perspectives?
  - How complex, significant, and controversial is this shift of organizational culture?
  - How are groups of your stakeholders likely to influence each other and their responses to this change?
  - What messaging about the change should be created?
  - How will the change be framed by others?
  - How will input be solicited from stakeholders about the change and the methods and manner of implementation?
  - What support needs to be in place to enable progress to be made in activating the change, monitoring the change process, and assessing change outcomes?

BUILDING STRATEGIC LISTENING INFRASTRUCTURE

- What channels and technologies need to be in place to support a listening culture?
  - Which stakeholders need new or improved channels for communication?
  - What channels will support strategic listening in each of these areas? What specific purpose will each channel support? Who will be accountable for monitoring and analyzing input received through new channels?
- What new roles and responsibilities need to be created to support a strategic listening culture?
  - Will knowledge and information workers be needed?
  - Will facilitators for groups, meetings, and input sessions be needed?
  - Will competitive intelligence experts be needed?

- Will ombudspersons be needed?
- Will listening trainers be needed?
- What training, resources, and support will people in these new roles need?
- What methods will be adopted to ensure continual monitoring of new listening practices, activities, and roles?
  - What methods from the listening appraisal can be adopted on a regular basis to keep a pulse reading of listening outcomes?

BUILDING STRATEGIC
LISTENING ROUTINES AND PRACTICES

- What scaffolding will be necessary to routinize strategic listening practices?
  - What templates, models, rubrics, and reminders can be used to initially build new routines?
  - How can role-playing, drills, and supporting materials be used to prompt effective listening routines and reinforce training about strategic listening?
  - What materials can be created to reinforce strategic listening in various daily scenarios? What is the best method to deliver opportunities for employees to practice responding in different listening contexts?
    - What materials would help guide strategic listening in internal meetings?
    - What materials would help guide strategic listening in external meetings?
    - What materials would help guide strategic listening with clients/customers?
    - What materials would help guide strategic listening with problematic situations (conflict and reports of wrongdoing)?
    - What materials would help guide strategic listening with environmental scanning and competitive intelligence surveillance?
    - What materials would help guide strategic listening with employee entry and exit?
    - What materials would help guide strategic listening in situations where diversity issues are prevalent?
    - What materials would help guide strategic listening with "non-friendlies"?
- How can supervisors and leaders in the organization be prompted to evaluate and improve materials designed to guide strategic listening?

- What changes in listening protocols, habits, and practices will be needed during a crisis? How will these new practices be activated?
- How can after-action reviews and after-listening reflections be incorporated into major events, crises management, and crisis prevention?
- What should be on the organization's listening dashboard?

Index